P9-BYN-063

Picturing Hemingway

FREDERICK VOSS

With an essay by Michael Reynolds

Picturing Hemingway

A WRITER IN HIS TIME

SMITHSONIAN NATIONAL PORTRAIT GALLERY   Washington, D.C.

in association with

YALE UNIVERSITY PRESS   New Haven and London

An exhibition at the National Portrait Gallery,
Smithsonian Institution, Washington, D.C.,
June 18–November 7, 1999

Designed by Richard Hendel.
Set in Quadraat and Meta type by B. Williams & Associates
Printed in Hong Kong by C&C Offset Printing Co.

Library of Congress Cataloging-in-Publication Data
Voss, Frederick.
Picturing Hemingway : a writer in his time / Frederick Voss : with
an essay by Michael Reynolds.
        p.   cm.
"An exhibition at the National Portrait Gallery, Smithsonian
Institution, Washington, D.C., June 18–November 7, 1999"—T.p.
verso.
Includes bibliographical references and index.
ISBN 0-300-07926-5 (cloth : alk. paper)
1. Hemingway, Ernest, 1899–1961—Portraits—Exhibitions.
2. Authors, American—20th century—Portraits—Exhibitions.
I. Reynolds, Michael S., 1937—   . II. National Portrait Gallery
(Smithsonian Institution)   III. Title.
PS3515.E37Z9154   1999
813'.52—dc21
[B]   98-52550

A catalogue record for this book is available from
the British Library.
The paper in this book meets the guidelines for permanence
and durability of the Committee on Production Guidelines for
Book Longevity of the Council on Library Resources.

10 9 8 7 6 5 4 3 2 1

CONTENTS

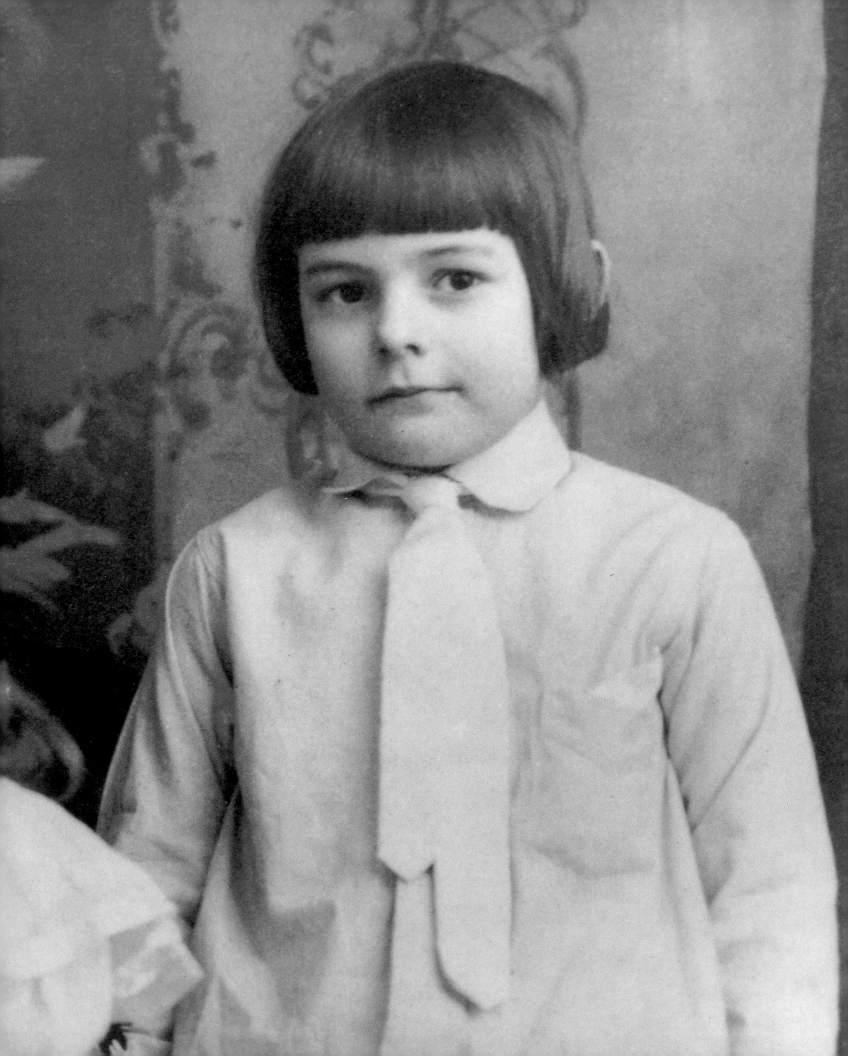

FOREWORD

At the National Portrait Gallery we are concerned with the art of portrayal. We are fascinated by the many ways in which painters, sculptors, graphic artists, and photographers have captured the likenesses of notables, and how the public has come to recognize its celebrities through these images. Some professions lend themselves well to portraiture. Actors and politicians are on stage by choice, and often they have taken pains to create a character for themselves through their dress, their posture, their familiar gestures, and their "public" expression. Others, like writers, are sometimes more elusive.

Herman Melville was very rarely the subject of a portrait, and to this day his likeness has eluded us at the Gallery. Some writers' portraits proclaim with great clarity that they wish to remain aloof, even if they submit to the painter's or photographer's request for a sitting. Henry James presents himself as lost in thought and enveloped in dignity, scarcely inviting us to know his inmost thoughts, though glad that we acknowledge his presence. The few images of Edgar Allan Poe, Henry David Thoreau, or Henry Wadsworth Longfellow give little clue—to my eye, at least—to the intellectual substance of their lives.

Not all writers are so rarely depicted, or so private. Certainly Ernest Hemingway is one of the most recognizable American writers of our century. Most Americans know his name, even if they have never read a word he has written; many can call to mind his grizzled, bearded countenance photographed in late middle age, and they know of his fondness for beautiful women, revelry, bullfighting, big-game hunting, and deep-sea fishing. How did this come about?

Partly, one imagines, because Hemingway led a genuinely interesting and varied life: going off to Paris when it was good to be an American expatriate there, serving as a correspondent during the Spanish civil war and World War II, and managing to combine the life of a writer with the pursuits of an avid sportsman. And partly it came about because he seems to have cultivated his public image with some care, comporting himself in appropriately manly fashion, keeping company with glamorous companions, and always seeming to be where the action was. The caricaturist Miguel Covarrubias painted for *Vanity Fair* an unforgettably acerbic image in 1933, showing Hemingway, clad in a leopard-skin loincloth, a hunting knife tucked in its waist, applying hair-growing ointment to his chest. In a moment of Victorian squeamishness, the magazine never published the caricature; had it done so, it would have been greeted with surprise by many who found the writer's virility so integral to his public persona.

Frederick Voss, who has assembled this visual biography of Hemingway, suggests that both the writer's own impulse to save everything documenting his life and the visual archive created by his mother (who produced a six-volume album of his childhood in Oak Park, Illinois) have made the iconographic record of Hemingway's career more abundant than that of just about any other American author. The selection from that record found in this volume, especially when examined alongside essays by Mr. Voss and the distinguished Hemingway biographer Michael Reynolds, thus offers an unusually effective evocation of the personality and accomplishments of one of the twentieth century's most noteworthy writers.

Unlike a John Steinbeck or a Sinclair Lewis, Hemingway was not inclined to explore large contemporary public issues or to use his fiction to create panoramic commentaries on society. Instead, his focus was largely on the individual's timeless struggle to survive and to find personal meaning in the world's inhospitable environment. Above all, he was a storyteller who sought to present his tales with a deliberate simplicity uniquely his own. In the process he took prose into a new realm that would have a lasting influence on countless writers to come, not only in America but around the world. I hope that this study of Hemingway will encourage readers to return to his work—or read it for the first time—and to experience the magnitude of that accomplishment.

ALAN FERN, director
National Portrait Gallery

ACKNOWLEDGMENTS

Any acknowledgments for a commemoration of Ernest Hemingway's one hundredth birthday must start with Hemingway himself. Because he was sometimes prickly when people expressed interest in his life, I am not sure how warmly he would have embraced this venture. In any case, he would have no one but himself to blame. For no American writer has ever left a richer and more engaging visual record of his career, and not to have used the occasion of his centennial to bring some of that archive together in book and exhibition form would have been a grave oversight indeed.

The largest portion of the Hemingway archive is in the care of the John F. Kennedy Library and Museum, and little would have been possible without the wonderful cooperation of its staff. A special debt is owed Steve Plotkin, curator of the Hemingway collection at the Kennedy, and Alan Goodrich, chief of its audiovisual division. They could not have been more helpful. Yet another important repository of Hemingway material is the Princeton University Library, and I am grateful as well for all the help that Dr. Don Skemer and other Special Collections staff provided during my visits there.

I also take this occasion to offer profound thanks to Michael Reynolds. In spite of a busy schedule that included finishing the final installment of his five-volume biography of Hemingway, he consented to collaborate in this enterprise, and the National Portrait Gallery is honored to be able to feature his insightful essay in this book.

Among the Gallery staff shaping this venture, three of the most important were Curator of Exhibitions Beverly Cox, Assistant Curator of Exhibitions Claire Kelly, and Exhibition Coordinator Liza Karvellas. A more efficient and encouraging trio of musem professionals would be hard to find. I also offer thanks to Heather Egan for her part in putting the manuscript for this book into presentable order and to Publications Officer Frances Stevenson and Managing Editor Dru Dowdy for their editorial expertise and publishing oversight. Finally, much gratitude goes to the museum's designers, Nello Marconi and Al Elkins, for their indispensable role for making the exhibition a reality.

LENDERS TO THE EXHIBITION

COMMERCE GRAPHICS LTD., INC., East Rutherford, New Jersey

ALBERT J. DEFAZIO III

HARRY RANSOM HUMANITIES RESEARCH CENTER,

    The University of Texas at Austin

JOHN F. KENNEDY LIBRARY, Boston

LIBRARY OF CONGRESS, Washington, D.C.

LIBRARY OF THE NATIONAL PORTRAIT GALLERY AND THE NATIONAL

    MUSEUM OF AMERICAN ART, SMITHSONIAN INSTITUTION,

    Washington, D.C.

NATIONAL PORTRAIT GALLERY, SMITHSONIAN INSTITUTION,

    Washington, D.C.

OGUNQUIT MUSEUM OF AMERICAN ART, Maine

MICHAEL PEIRCE

PRINCETON UNIVERSITY LIBRARY, New Jersey

PRIVATE COLLECTION

CHARLES SCRIBNER III

Hemingway as American Icon

HEMINGWAY AS AMERICAN ICON

MICHAEL REYNOLDS

American iconography is an open book—names and faces we have chosen to serve as shorthand references for a time, an event, or a quality of character that we find admirable. That these figures are remembered tells us something about our collective psychic needs, for none of them planned to be an American icon. To achieve widespread recognition in one's own time is crucial to the process, but the status of icon does not necessarily follow. Woodrow Wilson was once as widely recognized a political face as we had, but today he is reduced to a name in a long list of names, a historical figure but not an icon. To reach that higher level of recognition, one must last longer than the brief fret and strut allowed him. Abe Lincoln became such an icon: Honest Abe the uncommon common man, emancipation proclaimer, savior of the Union, martyr. We put his face on the copper penny, where the poorest of the poor see it daily. We put Alexander Hamilton on the ten-dollar bill, but today few would recognize his face on a magazine cover.

Some, like Charles Lindbergh, achieve such status through one daring act, one perfectly performed moment. Others reach it through notoriety, like Billy the Kid. We remember and recognize statesmen (Jefferson, Franklin, the two Roosevelts), military men (Washington, Lee, Custer, Eisenhower), athletes (Dempsey, Ruth, Jesse Owens, Muhammad Ali), entertainers (Marilyn Monroe, John Wayne, Louis Armstrong), but few and far between are the American writers whose faces remain in the public domain long after their deaths. Emerson, Dickinson, James, O'Neill, Dos Passos, Eliot, Faulkner, Fitzgerald, and Ellison were all important writers whose names may carry some vestige of their once-famous presence, but today not one man on the street out of a hundred would recognize any of these writers without an identifying caption. From our literary pantheon only a handful have reached the status of icon: Whitman, Poe, Twain, Hemingway—each of whom crystallized something new to American letters. Whitman is the fountainhead of American poetry, Poe of American horror, Twain of American humor. Hemingway is the modern voice, and of these four, only his name and face carry multiple and often contradictory connotations.

Born in 1899, Ernest Hemingway imprinted himself deeply into the literature, culture, and psyche of an America that was changing from an upstart nation into a world power. The generation of the 1890s—Fitzgerald, Faulkner, Dos Passos, and Hemingway—changed forever how Americans wrote about themselves and how others saw us. Disillusioned by the Great European War of 1914, these writers and their contemporaries became the Modernists of the 1920s. Among them, none was more prominent than Ernest Hemingway. Seventy years after the last roar of the 1920s, Hemingway's face still requires no identifying caption, for he became and remains an icon of our times, as well recognized in Shanghai as in Grand Forks.

In his frenetic public and private life, Hemingway had the uncanny ability to be always on the edge of whatever important was about to happen. After sustaining a serious war wound in 1918, he took us in his fiction and journalism to all the wars that followed: the Greco-Turkish war, 1922; the Spanish civil war, 1937; the Japanese invasion of China, 1941; the Normandy invasion, 1944. For a nation of increasingly city-bound spectators, Hemingway's life became a media event. He took us into Africa to hunt dangerous game, out onto the Gulf Stream to fish for marlin. He was a living example of America's promise: the young boy from Oak Park who set out to become the best writer of his time. With pluck and luck, talent and wit, hard work and hard living, he staked a credible claim to being just that. In the process he told us that pursuit was happiness, that one man alone was no fucking good, and that any story followed far enough would end badly. Before he burned out, he remodeled the American short story, changed the way characters talk, confronted the moral strictures confining the writer, and left behind a shelf of books telling us how we were in the first half of this century. In this year of his centennial, and as our century ends, it is fitting that we take a closer look at this icon of many meanings, Ernest Hemingway.

His friend Scott Fitzgerald once said that it was almost impossible to believe in the youth of one's parents; the same might be said about the youth of Ernest Hemingway, who grew so media tall that it is hard to think of him as a young man in Paris, magnetic, brash, and bawdy, a writer on the edge of immortality. Later, speaking of himself, he would say it was always a mistake to know an author well. There were those who agreed, remembering him in all his flaws; others, no matter how badly he hurt them, never ceased to defend him. This literary pushing and shoving, which began early, did not thrive until he was dead and famous among his survivors. For some, he was the most important event in their lives. For others, he was only a summer storm crossing the bay. But no matter how he touched them, not the least of his commentators ever forgot the feel or look of him, never forgot the way he could exhaust the oxygen by simply walking into the room.

Women, those who loved him and those who did not, remembered him in great detail. One woman said, "I wouldn't have been surprised at anything Ernest did. He was unexpected and temperamental, a lovable person who took a great deal of understanding. He was sensitive, although he didn't seem to be. If you didn't know him well, you'd think he was rather tough." His first wife remembered him as "one of the most sensitive people I ever heard of, and easily hurt." She also said, "He had the nerve of a brass monkey." He was "the kind of man to whom men, women, and dogs were attracted. He was scornful of some people and would say outrageous things about them. He had a cruel streak. Yet his kindness went just about as far in the other direction."[1] Kitty Cannell thought him phony, pretentious, and untrustworthy, but she could not forget his apple cheeks, his infectious grin, or his boyish enthusiasms.[2]

The men drawn to him had difficulty performing at his level of intensity, for Hemingway did nothing halfheartedly. Many enjoyed the bullfights, but few followed them as he did all summer in Spain. Skiing, fishing, or drinking, he was competitive always. "He liked to win everything," Mike Strater complained long afterward.[3] For Gerald Murphy, who could not compete with the younger man so charming to his wife, the encounter with Hemingway changed him forever. He found the writer "huge and forceful, and he overstated everything and talked so rapidly and so graphically and so well that you found yourself agreeing with him."[4] Whether it was the bullfights at Pamplona, the ski slopes at Schruns, or an evening at a Paris dance hall, the Hemingway experience always demanded unexpected emotional resources. Few of his male friendships in those early days lasted longer than five years. Reading the letters, one can watch them burn up and out like incandescent lights. To whatever he touched in those days he added scale and a sense of importance. Murphy said, "The lives of some of us will seem, I suppose by comparison, piddling. . . . For me, he has the violence and excess of genius."[5] It is not given to many men to imprint themselves so deeply upon their generation as did Ernest Hemingway in the first half of this century. Although he did not outlive his friends and enemies, who got in their last words, he burned so much more brightly than most that we still read their statements by his light.

We know so well the icon he became that it is difficult to imagine him unfledged, vibrant with energy, laughing and joking along the boulevards of Paris. Wearing sneakers, old trousers, and a patched jacket, his long hair sticking out from under his cap, he was six feet tall, broad shouldered, mustached, and handsome, setting his own style. When the occasion demanded, he could put on his one tweed suit with its dark tie, but he never owned a summer straw hat in an age when only the poorest American was without one. For Nathan Asch, "It was an event when this towering figure passed the sidewalk tables at the Dôme. Arms waved in greeting and friends ran out to urge him to sit down with them. . . . He wouldn't quite recognize whoever greeted him. Then suddenly his beautiful smile appeared that made those watching him also smile."[6] Continuously moving with his curious, slow-footed gait, he was a man on his way somewhere else, always.

Today Hemingway's name and face appear in strange and diverse places. More than a few problem drinkers salute Ernest as a patron saint without ever having read his fiction. At mahogany bars in Key West, Bimini, Havana, Madrid, and Paris, one still finds faces who claim to have shared a drink with Ernest, to have been at the bar the night he said such and such. At the Floridita in Havana, there is the infamous "Papa Doble" daiquiri; at the Paris Ritz Hotel, there is a Hemingway Bar; and hardly a metropolitan area is without a restaurant called A Moveable Feast. Paramilitarists use Hemingway quotes as personal sign-offs on e-mail: *There is no hunting like the hunting of man and those who have hunted armed men long enough and liked it, never really care for anything else thereafter.*[7] Big-game hunters, marlin fishermen, boxing enthusiasts, and hard-core journalists claim Hemingway as "one of us." Once-party-line Communists and staunch Republicans find elements in Hemingway that support their Weltanschauung. In 1992 in Moscow I gathered with Soviet scholars who knew our man from Oak Park as well as I did. In what was then the USSR, a 600,000-copy edition of *For Whom the Bell Tolls* sold out within a year. In the last decade I have been invited to a Hemingway conference in the heart of China and have been visited by a Fulbright scholar from Japan, where there is a thriving Hemingway Society.

I would like to believe that this incredible recognition is due to Hemingway's fiction, and to some degree it is. In 1989, on the television game show *Jeopardy!* there was a Hemingway category that included a question about his little-known play *The Fifth Column*. The *Jeopardy!* contestant knew the play was about the Spanish civil war. I was amazed, but then I am continually amazed by Hemingway's longevity. What other American author has five of his houses preserved in three states and one foreign country? What other author has a street named for him in Pamplona, a line of sporting goods in New York, a look-alike contest in Key West, a fishing contest in Havana, an annual PEN literary award, and a bad-writing contest in Venice? Can you imagine a William Faulkner look-alike contest? Can you imagine the decorous T. S. Eliot lending his name from the grave to a line of fastidious somber suits? When I think of Eliot, all I can see are his beautiful lines of poetry lingering always as sounds within my head, but I can't see Eliot the man. The Possum, as Pound called him, has disappeared from view. But not so with Hemingway, who continues to walk amongst us, refusing stubbornly to die.

Unfortunately, the image we have permanently embedded in our collective consciousness is the Old Hemingway, the one definitively captured in the Karsh portrait. The Key West look-alike contest honors this old man, not the Hemingway of the 1930s, when he lived in that once peaceful outpost. He did not begin as the writer at sixty, nor was his rise to fame instantaneous. It began in Paris in 1921, when Hemingway arrived unknown and unpublished, but bearing introductions from Sherwood Anderson to the already cult Left Bank figures. With Ezra Pound as his mentor, Sylvia Beach as his friend, and Gertrude Stein as his surrogate mother and godmother to his son, Hemingway was as well connected as a want-to-be writer could be. Pound got him to work as an unpaid assistant for Ford Madox Ford, who was then publishing the short-lived but important *transatlantic review*. From that vantage point, Ernest connected with every expatriate American writer in Paris. Through Stein's salon, he fell in love with Cézanne's landscapes and met young painters on the rise—Juan Gris, Joan Miró, Pablo Picasso. At Beach's bookshop and lending library, he extended his education and his circle of acquaintances: George Antheil, Adrienne Monnier, Archibald MacLeish, James Joyce.

By 1924 there were rumors floating at the Cafés Dôme and Select that the handsome young man from Oak Park was thought by insiders to be a writer of promise. Little and obscure magazines were beginning to publish some of his poetry, which was read by the smart set in the East Village. Before any of the New York crowd recognized his face, they were quoting his lines:

> I know monks masturbate at night,
> That pet cats screw,
> That some girls bite,
> And yet
> What can I do
> To set things right?[8]

The American painter Henry "Mike" Strater was painting portraits of Ernest, and in 1924 Scott Fitzgerald, before ever meeting Ernest, wrote his editor at Scribner "about a young man named Ernest Hemmingway [*sic*] who lives in Paris . . . & has a brilliant future."[9] Over the next two years, Hemingway published three books, two of which more than fulfilled Fitzgerald's prediction. The short stories from *In Our Time* (1925) became American classics before their author was thirty-two. His discovery of the feria of San Fermin in Pamplona, Spain, resulted in his roman à clef, *The Sun Also Rises* (1926), making him the epitome of the expatriate American writing on the Left Bank.

Leaving all his mentors behind—Anderson, Stein, Pound—Hemingway, his college-equivalent education completed, was quitting Paris just as the first impression of him as expatriate was forming. He was never an expatriate, he later insisted, only a writer living cheaply in Paris. His generation, he said, was never "lost"—beat up by the war, but not lost. Hemingway also asked his New York publisher Scribner to stop putting out biographical information about him: he wanted his private life to remain that way. But it was too late. When he divorced his first wife, the story appeared in the *New York Times*. Photographs, caricatures, and line drawings and woodcuts of his handsome face were not yet ubiquitous in American journals, but they were well placed: the *New York Times Book Review*, *Vanity Fair*, *Bookman*, *Town and Country*. Young, handsome, virile, and talented, he was a contradiction: the active man who excelled at the contemplative life of letters. Book reviewers spoke of his writing in phrases uncommon in the previous age: "Hemingway has a lean, pleasing, tough resilience. His language is fibrous and athletic, colloquial and fresh, hard and clean."[10] "His phrases are brittle, with mordant edges. . . . In lean, spare sentences he always makes you see the thing he writes about."[11] "Any future anthology of the American short story which does not include 'The Killers' will not be complete."[12]

In 1930, with a new best-seller—*A Farewell to Arms*—making his name more commonplace, Hemingway moved to Key West, Florida, just as the Great Depression was rearranging the face of America. A more remote location would have been difficult to find, as would a less expensive one. Key West was half-empty, down on its luck, and on the verge of bankruptcy—an ideal base of operations for a writer. Between 1930 and 1936, in and out of Key West, Hemingway created a new writer for the different times. While proletariat writers, their names now long forgotten, were writing of textile mill strikes, Hemingway gave us *Death in the Afternoon*, a natural history of the Spanish bullfight as well as a statement about the responsibilities of the artist. When Key West allowed the Federal Emergency Relief Act to take over the management of the devastated fishing port, Hemingway published *Green Hills of Africa*, a safari book, a book of aesthetics, a writer's book. Going against the grain of the leftist literary thirties, Hemingway was ever his own man, never another face in the crowd. His novels were being translated into French and German; *A Farewell to Arms* became a movie starring Gary Cooper. Hemingway's writing was being regularly imitated and parodied in prominent places. "Death in the Rumble Seat" appeared in the *New Yorker* with the disclaimer: "With the usual apologies to Ernest Hemingway, who must be pretty sick of this sort of thing."[13]

While Depression-era Hollywood gave us escapist films in which the gentlemen wore tuxedos, Hemingway was writing a series of personal essays, called "Letters," for the newly founded men's magazine *Esquire*. His subject matter was himself in situ: Africa, the Gulf Stream, Paris, Spain, Cuba, Key West, wherever his interests took him. These informal essays were frequently interlarded with equally informal photos of the author in action at sea, or on the Serengeti. Brawny, bearded in a clean-shaven America, bare-chested, he was who he was, and we loved him for it. Single-handedly, he became a spectator sport for increasingly sedentary Americans. When he boated a 468-pound black marlin, *Time* magazine showed us the photograph.[14] When he returned from his African safari, New York reporters were waiting at dockside, flashbulbs popping.[15] Wherever he went, whatever he did—fish, hunt, brawl, travel, marry, or write—the media were close at hand. His *Esquire* voice was personal and frequently humorous, combative, or prophetic. In September 1935 he warned his audience about the next war, which he said would begin within two years. In September 1937 he was in Madrid reporting on the Spanish civil war. That October, Hemingway was on the cover of *Time* and his last experimental work from the Key West years—*To Have and Have Not*—was published. Without a public relations team, without even a literary agent to push his case, Hemingway during the 1930s gained the kind of public recognition usually reserved for movie stars and national politicians. His 1930s ended with his first play—*The Fifth Column*—opening on Broadway and his best-seller, *For Whom the Bell Tolls,* featured by Book-of-the-Month Club and bought by more than half a million Americans. *Life* magazine documented the novel with photographs from the Spanish civil war, and the story of the dynamiter and the partisans quickly became a film with Gary Cooper and the very young Ingrid Bergman. When Hemingway met her on approval for the role, *Life* featured them with two pages of photographs.[16]

For the next ten years and at the height of his astonishing career, Hemingway published no fiction at all, yet when *Saturday Review of Literature* polled its readers in 1944, he was voted the leading American novelist by a two-to-one margin.[17] His name was now being dropped regularly in the syndicated columns of Earl Wilson and Leonard Lyons. When he went to World War II as a *Collier's* reporter, his own activities became news: "Hemingway Is Injured," "Hemingway Captures Six," "A Close Hemingway Call," "Hemingway's Son Captured," "Hemingway Still at Front," "Hemingway's Son Is Liberated."

Between June and December 1944, Hemingway covered the European war with manic energy, deliberately putting himself in dangerous situations. On D-Day, June 6, 1944, rather than observe the Normandy landing from the relative safety of the correspondents' ship, Hemingway went aboard a landing craft to get a closer view. The result was his essay "Voyage to Victory," which remains vintage Hemingway:

> I saw a ragged shell hole through the steel plates forward of her pilothouse where an 88-mm. German shell had punched through. Blood was dripping from the shiny edges of the hole into the sea with each roll of the LCI. Her rails and hull had been befouled by seasick men, and her dead were laid forward of her pilothouse.[18]

At the end of that month, he flew twice on Royal Air Force missions intercepting German rockets headed for England. In July he was attached briefly to George Patton's Third Army before transferring to Colonel Charles "Buck" Lanham's Twenty-Second Regiment of the Fourth Army. By August, when *Collier's* published "London Fights the Robots," Hemingway was leading a small group of French irregulars and unattached GIs toward the liberation of Paris and the Ritz Bar.

In and out of Paris all that fall, Hemingway alternated between the battlefields of France and a bedroom at the Ritz, where his affair with Mary Welsh Monk was proceeding as well as the war effort. When he was not sick with colds and sore throats or suffering from recurring headaches from a severe concussion he had sustained in London, Hemingway was by turns brave, gentle, obsessive, foolhardy, loving, and brutal: a man surfing along the edge of his manic drive. That fall *Collier's* published his two essays "Battle for Paris" and "How We Came to Paris."

Between 1945 and 1961 whatever private life Hemingway had maintained disappeared completely. Although he was now living outside of Havana, Cuba, he was constantly sought out by reporters, columnists, war buddies, baseball players, college sophomores, and a new breed of academics who were teaching his fiction and publishing scholarly articles about it. When his fourth wife, Mary Welsh, suffered an almost fatal tubular pregnancy in rather remote Casper, Wyoming, the story was in the *New York Times* the next morning.[19] When Hemingway hunted ducks or went to Italy on vacation, *Time* reported it. In January 1949 millions of *Life* readers absorbed Malcolm Cowley's sixteen-page biographic essay, "A Portrait of Mister Papa," with its accompanying photographs: Hemingway as boxer, as war correspondent, as drinking man, much-married man, and wounded man. Between 1941 and 1961 *Life* published sixteen feature stories on Hemingway, more than any literary agent could have arranged.[20]

By this time Hemingway was larger than life, a legendary figure whose exploits, real and otherwise, were widely known. As John Raeburn has so accurately noted: "Because so many untruths commonly permeated talk about Hemingway's life, distinguishing fact from fiction became nearly impossible. . . . The more improbable the tale, the greater currency it had, and the fabrications tended to eclipse the truth."[21] In 1950 Lillian Ross's famous profile of Hemingway came out in the *New Yorker*, and his new novel *Across the River and into the Trees* was published to conflicting reviews but solid sales. E. B. White favored him with a parody: "Across the Street and Into the Grill."[22] Would-be biographers, knocking at his door, he tended off like a good general fighting a rear-guard action, giving up ground reluctantly and wisely.

Just when the critics were ready to write Hemingway off as past his prime, he published *The Old Man and the Sea* in *Life*, with his own stern visage on the cover.[23] By the 1950s his work was being translated into all of the world's major languages. When his airplane crashed on the 1953–54 return to Africa, his obituary ran worldwide; friends and passing acquaintances wrote of their close encounters with the man. Then, miraculously it seemed, he was alive, only to crash a second time during the rescue. Seriously hurt, but on his feet, Hemingway fulfilled all the expectations of his following. Later that year, he was canonized with the Nobel Prize for literature.

Time and again during the postwar period, Hollywood turned his fiction into film: *The Sun Also Rises, The Killers, To Have and Have Not, The Macomber Affair, The Snows of Kilimanjaro, The Old Man and the Sea*. At the same time, his short stories were being transformed into television productions. This media attention to his writing produced even more intrusion into his life. By the time of his suicide in 1961 (a two-week-running story in almost every major newspaper of the world), we had used him up. As Auden wrote on the death of Yeats: "He became his admirers." The poet might have added "and his detractors." From the grave, however, Hemingway published *A Moveable Feast, Islands in the Stream, Garden of Eden,* and *The Dangerous Summer.* This year, thirty-eight years since his death, we are promised the last of the unpublished manuscripts—his African journal from 1953–54.

A quick count of my bookshelf shows eighteen full or partial biographies of Hemingway the man and the writer. His houses are preserved in Oak Park (two), Key West, Ketchum, and Cuba. Each summer at San Fermin, thousands of admirers drink themselves silly along the Pamplona *camino* that bears Hemingway's name and leads to the bullring. A recent issue of *Time,* selecting the one hundred most important artists and entertainers of this century, featured six writers: James Joyce, Franz Kafka, T. S. Eliot, Virginia Woolf, Ralph Ellison, and Ernest Hemingway. To be identified by that magazine's readers, the first five now need a caption. Thirty years after his death, Hemingway still does not. To achieve and maintain this level of public recognition is more rare than winning the Nobel Prize, more elusive than great fortune, and perfectly in keeping with Hemingway's mantra: *Il faut (d'abord) durer.* First one must endure. This year of his centennial, there will be pilgrimages to the various Hemingway sites, the faithful armed with guidebooks to Hemingway's Paris, Hemingway's Key West. There will be more stories, television documentaries, celebrations, and depreciations, all of which will reinforce his name and face as American icon.

To become such an icon is a mixed blessing in our time, for the ravenous public quickly sucks the real man dry. No matter how resilient he seemed in the media, Hemingway aged quickly, and the image that he in part created was a difficult one to maintain in the face of failing health. No one sets the pedestal of national icon as his or her goal, certainly not Hemingway. He wanted to be the best writer of his generation; he wanted his writing to last forever. He also wanted to live the strenuous life as preached by his childhood idol, Teddy Roosevelt, the icon of American manliness at the turn of the last century. All of this he achieved through his own efforts. His was the Horatio Alger story writ large: the unknown young man with only a high school education who made himself into one of the most admired and imitated writers of his century. He became who he wanted to be, and we, the American public, made him into an icon, a representative of either a writing style or a lifestyle that we admired, envied, desired, and knew we would never have. He took the risks we could not afford; played the game for which we lacked the skills; sustained the hurts that we avoided; and wrote the stories that moved us.

Like most enduring icons, in relative obscurity he was formed into the pure product, the drop of distillate that floats on the surface, intense and self-contained. Slowly it spreads, becoming thinner and thinner, until it covers the entire surface. Some remember the initial intensity, but they die out, leaving us to our easy generalizations about the icon. Thus we have Hemingway the hunter, Hemingway the self-reliant, Hemingway the fisherman, the boxer, the lover, the warrior, and almost as an afterthought, Hemingway the writer. In spite of wars, injuries, mental and physical illness, and his strenuous life, Hemingway left, permanently embedded in our literary history, several of the finest short stories written in this century, at least three major novels, and a writer's life carried out on an epic scale. We read his works the same way a surveyor reads geodetic benchmarks: it does not matter whether we like the elevation or not, or admire the view; at least we know exactly where we are. His clean, well-lighted style has, at some point, influenced most American writers of this century. That he self-destructed affirmed his humanity; that he wrote as well as he did promises his permanence. Whether one admires Hemingway or not, he is an authentic artifact, a piece of the continent, an American author whose career changed the face of our fiction. Those who know little of his life and less of his writing call him "macho," a word he never used. Those more knowledgeable appreciate the complexity of the man whose message was simple and true: *We are doomed to lose, so we must lose on our own terms. It is all that is left us, we exiles from the garden of Eden.*

NOTES

1. Denis Brian, *The True Gen: An Intimate Portrait of Ernest Hemingway by Those Who Knew Him* (New York: Grove, 1988), pp. 52–55.

2. Kathleen Cannell to Bernard Saranson, private collection.

3. Brian, *True Gen*, p. 49.

4. Honoria Murphy Donnelly, *Sara and Gerald* (New York: Holt, Rinehart, and Winston, 1983), p. 165.

5. Gerald Murphy to Sara Murphy, September 4–9, 1937, *Letters from the Lost Generation*, ed. Linda Patterson Miller, pp. 199–200.

6. Brian, *True Gen*, p. 54.

7. Ernest Hemingway, "On the Blue Water: A Gulf Stream Letter" *Esquire* (April 1936), pp. 184–85.

8. Ernest Hemingway, "The Earnest Liberal's Lament," *Querschnitt* (autumn 1924), p. 231.

9. F. Scott Fitzgerald to Max Perkins, October 10, 1924, *A Life in Letters*, ed. Matthew J. Bruccoli and Judith S. Baughman, p. 82.

10. *New York Times Book Review* (October 18, 1925), p. 8.

11. *Kansas City Star* (December 12, 1925).

12. *Town and Country* (December 15, 1927), p. 59.

13. Walcott Gibbs, *New Yorker* (October 8, 1932), p. 15.

14. *Time* (July 24, 1933), p. 24.

15. *New York Herald Tribune* (April 4, 1934).

16. *Life* (February 24, 1941), pp. 48, 51.

17. *Saturday Review of Literature* (August 5, 1944), p. 61.

18. "Voyage to Victory," reprinted in *By-Line Ernest Hemingway* (New York: Scribner, 1967), p. 351.

19. *New York Times* (August 21, 1946).

20. John Raeburn, *Fame Became of Him: Hemingway as Public Writer* (Bloomington: Indiana University Press, 1984), pp. 129–33.

21. Ibid., p. 23.

22. *New Yorker* (October 14, 1950), p. 28.

23. *Life* (September 1, 1952).

Picturing Ernest Hemingway

By the time Ernest Hemingway died in 1961, he had achieved a popular fame perhaps unrivaled in the history of American letters. His lean storytelling style had influenced a generation of writers around the world. Some of his works had assumed the stature of classics practically from the moment they reached print, and there were those who argued that he was the greatest American writer of the twentieth century. But professional achievements were not the only ingredients of his reputation. Ruggedly handsome, he had led a life filled with exploits that seemed to imbue him with a virile glamour more usually reserved for the likes of an Errol Flynn or Gary Cooper. As an ambulance driver in World War I, he had been wounded and decorated, and he was a front-line correspondent during both the Spanish civil war and World War II. He was an aficionado of bullfighting and, in his youth, had even tested his own mettle in that ancient blood sport in amateur free-for-alls; he had killed big game on African safaris; he had been in two airplane crashes within thirty-six hours and lived to read his own obituaries; he was an expert deep-sea fisherman. It was not, however, merely what he did that accounted for his public image; it was also fed by legend-making exaggerations and out-and-out fabrications that frequently crept into stories about him and that he himself sometimes encouraged. But whether it was grounded in truth or fiction, Hemingway's personal reputation as the all-around man of action ultimately eclipsed his own widely revered fiction. As one observer put it in 1954, he was "a more fabulous character than any he ever created," and even for many Americans who had never read a word of his prose or had little notion of the whys of his literary prominence, he was an eminently familiar cultural presence in their lives.[1]

Wound up in the story of Hemingway's rise to literary celebrity are the visual images of him—several paintings, some drawings, and many, many hundreds of photographs. The pictorial record of his career is exceptionally rich and encompasses just about every significant stage of it. In fact, it may well be that, pictorially speaking, Hemingway is the best-documented writer in all of American letters. Given this visual plenitude, anything approaching comprehensive treatment of Hemingway images is impossible here, and the discussion that follows examines the circumstances and significance of but a comparative handful of these images.

Among the most compelling early likenesses are a pair of small oil portraits that date from late 1922 or early 1923 and that were the work of Henry Strater (figures 1 and 2). During his undergraduate days at Princeton, the Kentucky-born Strater had been a friend of F. Scott Fitzgerald's, and he eventually became the model for the nonconforming Burne Holiday in Fitzgerald's first novel, *This Side of Paradise*. A student of French painter Édouard Vuillard, he had drawn considerable praise for his *Nude with Dog* at the Paris Salon d'automne of 1922. That success drew Strater into the orbit of the poet Ezra Pound, which Hemingway had also entered several months earlier. Soon Pound was recruiting Strater to do the illustrations for the publication of a section of his major work, *The Cantos*.

1

Henry Strater's first portrait of Hemingway

Henry Strater (1896–1987), oil on panel, 55.9 x 42.5 cm (22 x 16¾ in.), 1922/1923. Permanent Collection, Ogunquit Museum of American Art, Maine; gift of the artist

opposite

2

Henry Strater's second portrait of Hemingway (The Boxer Portrait)

Henry Strater (1896–1987), oil on board, 32.3 x 23.5 cm (12¾ x 9¼ in.), 1922/1923. Permanent Collection, Ogunquit Museum of American Art, Maine; gift of the artist

"Portrait of
Ernest
Hemingway"

H. Strater, '22.

Rapallo, Italy

Strater and Hemingway had much in common. Both had come to Paris in 1921 with much the same thought in mind—that this center of European culture and home of an ever-enlarging Anglo-American artistic community was a good place to further their professional ambitions. Like Hemingway, Strater had been an ambulance driver during World War I. He also shared Hemingway's passion for sports, especially boxing. Not long after the two first met at a favorite Parisian hangout for American expatriate intellectuals, the Café du Dôme, they became frequent sparring partners.

Determining with certainty just where and when Strater did his two portraits of Hemingway is almost impossible. The evidence that exists is contradictory on some very basic points. Both pictures bear the date 1922 in their lower right corners, and the inscription on one of them further states that it was done in Rapallo, Italy. In Strater's memoir, published in 1961, the artist said that he painted the two likenesses in quick succession in Hemingway's hotel room at Rapallo. He painted the profile portrait first, he said. But because Hemingway complained that it looked "'too literary, like H. G. Wells,'" Strater obligingly painted a second portrait, this time in full face. All of this testimony—the 1922 dating on both pictures and Strater's written account of the circumstances of their execution—seems to fit neatly together save for one crucial detail: although by late 1922 Strater was indeed in Rapallo, where he had gone to work with Pound on the *Cantos* illustrations, Hemingway was many miles away skiing in Switzerland, and he did not yield to Pound's urgings that he stop in Rapallo until mid-February of 1923.[2]

Any of several possible explanations may account for this discrepancy. The 1922 date on the portraits, for example, could have been added many years later by Strater when he was no longer clear about the year of their making. If, on the other hand, the portraits' datings are accurate, it must be that Strater misremembered in his late-life memoir the venue of Hemingway's sittings for the likenesses and that Hemingway instead posed for them at Strater's studio just outside Paris in fall 1922. But murkiness of the details about time and place does not diminish interest in Strater's two portraits as a record of Hemingway's first year or so in Paris. In the profile likeness, which Strater recollected painting first, a slightly hunched Hemingway appears keenly focused, as if he has shut out all the distractions of the world around him to concentrate solely on his own thoughts. Indeed, he seems to be in the very act of creating, and although the picture does not show what his downward gaze is fixed upon, it may well be a bit of writing that he has just completed. He also seems to be wearing an overcoat, which suggests that the room where he sits is uncomfortably cold. In a way, the image is as much genre as it is the portrait of a specific person, for although the picture is unmistakably of Hemingway, its overall mood transcends its subject to evoke a romantic, literary type—the solitary, comfort-deprived young artist, dedicated to perfecting his art.

As Strater claimed, Hemingway may not especially have liked being cast into that part at the time of the portrait's making. But interestingly enough, that was the very image he nostalgically cultivated much later in life in the semifictional reminiscences of his early Paris years, *A Moveable Feast*. It is thus easy to imagine the writer in Strater's portrait playing out a number of vignettes found in Hemingway's memoir. There was the cold, blustery day, for example, when he went to a Paris café instead of trying to heat up his chilly writing room, and there became so absorbed in the story he was writing that he lost all connection to his surroundings until it was done. Or there were the times he sat in solitude, looking out over the roofs of Paris, unable to make the words flow, and thinking to himself that what he must do now was "write the truest sentence that you know."[3]

This profile likeness also puts one in mind of a story that seems to have begun germinating in Hemingway's mind during his 1923 stay at Rapallo. "Cat in the Rain" is about an affection-starved woman, staying with her husband in a hotel, who focuses on a stray cat as the solution to her lonely plight. One quarter where she cannot obtain the emotional succor she so craves is her husband, who throughout the story remains too deeply engrossed in his reading to sense, much less ease, his wife's loneliness. If ever an editor went in search of an illustration for this tale to depict the detached husband wrapped up in his thoughts, he could have done no better than this portrait of its author.

Strater's second likeness of Hemingway, in full face, was much more pleasing to the subject, enough so that Hemingway wanted Strater to leave it to him in his will. It is not difficult to determine why Hemingway was taken with it. He was a man, after all, who placed great store in his virility, and behind so much of what ultimately gave shape to his public personality—his pursuit of hunting and boxing, his passion for bullfighting, his war reporting—there seemed to be an obsessive concern for asserting his masculinity. What Hemingway, in other words, liked most about the second Strater likeness was doubtless its sweatshirted maleness, especially when measured against the profile portrait, which had about it perhaps too strong a whiff of the effete poet for Hemingway's taste.

The second portrait may have appealed to Hemingway for yet another reason as well. For in its generalizing brushwork and elliptical treatment of features, it offered a pictorial equivalent of what he was beginning to try to do in his own art. Just as Strater had created a sense of him with only a minimal attention to detail, Hemingway was seeking a prose style capable of reducing his subject matter to its essentials. It was thus fitting when *in our time*, Hemingway's small collection of his early experiments along that line, appeared in early 1924 with a woodcut frontispiece portrait of him based on the second Strater likeness.

Strater remained a good Hemingway friend for a number of years, and in 1930 he painted a third portrait of him. After Hemingway moved to Key West, Florida, in the late 1920s, the artist frequently joined him there for fishing expeditions. Often Hemingway was more fun to be with than anybody Strater had ever known, but there were moments when the artist found the writer insufferably competitive and overbearing. After an outing off Bimini in 1935, when Strater claimed that Hemingway had intentionally spoiled his catch of a thousand-pound marlin, the friendship cooled. Ultimately, the relationship was reduced to an exchange of letters every few years.

In the first few weeks after Hemingway and his first wife, Hadley, took up residence in Paris, one of their happiest surprises was the discovery of a bookshop and lending library named Shakespeare and Company in the rue de l'Odéon. Opened in 1919 and owned by Sylvia Beach, the shop's specialty was books in English. By the time Hemingway found it on the morning of December 28, 1921, it was well on its way to becoming an important social crossroads for the city's Anglo-American expatriate community of writers.

Hemingway loved the place from the moment he stepped through its door, and later that day he came back with Hadley, eager to share his find with her. The shop's main attraction, of course, was its stock of books and literary magazines, which hinted to Hemingway of facets of literature as yet unknown to him. But he was also much taken with the shop's proprietor, who readily engaged him in conversation about himself. Beach, he recalled years later, had a lively face and well-shaped legs. Her greatest virtue, however, was her sympathetic companionability, and he claimed, "No one I ever knew was nicer to me."[4]

On his early visits to Beach's shop Hemingway must have noticed that the wall spaces not covered over with bookshelves were filled with photographic images of some of the era's most innovative British and American writers, such as James Joyce, T. S. Eliot, Ezra Pound, and Sherwood Anderson. The pictures were hung haphazardly. Running up the wall one above another, they were not always easy to view. Even so, they constituted a sort of hall of fame of avant-garde letters, and it probably struck Hemingway that to rate a place in this collection was a sign—if a small one—of admission into the literary fraternity.

In late 1921 no case could be made for Hemingway's inclusion in Shakespeare and Company's photographic pantheon. To the world at large, he was mainly a journalist, earning his living as a European features correspondent for the *Toronto Star*. As a man of letters, he could claim only some high aspirations and a stash of unpublished pieces written mostly in derivative, conventional styles. It remained to be seen whether those aspirations would be fulfilled.

By the onset of summer in 1923, however, Hemingway's literary worthiness had begun to emerge. In his year and a half in Paris, he had developed many connections among the city's Anglo-American literati and had become the protégé of two of that community's leading figures, Ezra Pound and Gertrude Stein. More important, Hemingway was about to have his first book published. *Three Stories & Ten Poems* was being brought out by a small press recently founded by Hemingway's fellow expatriate writer Robert McAlmon. The book was only sixty-four pages long, came out in an edition of three hundred, and hardly constituted a big splash in the publishing world. Nevertheless, within the Anglo-American literary community of Paris, it mattered. Locally speaking, Hemingway had begun to make good on his creative ambitions, and *Three Stories* was all the evidence needed to convince Sylvia Beach that it was time to make room for an image of him on her shop's walls.

The precise unveiling date of the portrait photograph at Shakespeare and Company is unknown (figure 3). But copies of *Three Stories* arrived there from the printer on August 13, 1923, and Hemingway and his wife stopped at the shop that day. They were heading in a few days to Toronto, where Hemingway expected to work for a while out of the *Star*'s headquarters—a move prompted by Hadley's pregnancy and a distrust of French doctors to deliver their baby safely. So Hemingway was there in part to say good-bye. He was also there to inspect with pride the volume of *Three Stories* featured in Beach's window and to pick up four author's copies credited to publisher McAlmon's account. It was probably on this visit that Hemingway presented Beach with a portrait photograph, inscribing it, "For Sylvia Beach / Ernest

For Sylvia Beach
Ernest Hemingway
M R Paris Aug. 1923

Hemingway / Aug. 1923." Not too long afterward the picture found its way into Beach's gallery of modern Anglo-American writers.

The maker of Beach's new Hemingway photograph was Man Ray. An American member of the avant-garde dadaist movement, which rejected the traditional rules of art in favor of the irrational, Ray moved to Paris in 1921, about five months ahead of Hemingway. He quickly made a place for himself among the city's dadaists, but he did not find much market for his paintings and assemblages. As a result, he fell back on his long-standing side interest in photography to support himself, and within a short time he had established a reputation as a skilled and creative portrait photographer. Among his clients was Sylvia Beach, who for a number of years frequently sent to his studio writers whose portrait photographs she wanted for her shop.

Man Ray remarked years later that his Hemingway likeness for Beach invested the writer with "a poetic look, making him very handsome besides."[5] The image also conveys a sense of confident self-possession, which might help to explain one of the more intriguing aspects of the early stages of Hemingway's rise to fame. Even before his talents were proven, he seemed to inspire remarkable convictions about his literary genius within the Parisian intellectual community. In late 1924, for example, when he was still a year away from producing a major volume of short stories and two years away from publication of his first novel, a critic in the Paris edition of the *Chicago Tribune* described him as "one of the most genuinely epic talents of any youngster writing in English today."[6] In handing down this judgment, the observer had, to be sure, some hard evidence to go on, but not much: the slender *Three Stories & Ten Poems* and an even slimmer volume of short descriptive vignettes, *in our time*. One cannot help but wonder whether this hyperbolic praise was shaped in part by the authoritative self-assurance recorded in Man Ray's photograph, an aura that led many who knew Hemingway during his early Paris years to accept his potential as an act of faith.

The compositional strength of Man Ray's 1923 portrait of Hemingway merits a place in the forefront of familiar Hemingway imagery. But outside of the patrons at Shakespeare and Company, very few ever saw it, and today the picture is among the least-known likenesses in the Hemingway iconography. Equally obscure is a portrait that Hemingway sat for in 1925, but which is nevertheless linked with the writer's first major professional triumph, the publication of *The Sun Also Rises* in 1926 (figure 4).

Many particulars about this pen-and-ink drawing are puzzling, and some can only be guessed at. The maker of the likeness, John Blomshield, is at best a shadowy figure. Trained at New York City's Art Students League, he went to Europe about 1923, and during his two- or three-year stay there he did some writing on early Italian Renaissance art and architecture for *Arts* magazine. Just how he met Hemingway and why he did his portrait in 1925 are both unclear, and not too long after the drawing was completed, he set out for India. Before leaving, he gave the drawing to Hemingway, inscribing it "To Ernest Hemingway / from John Blomshield / Paris 1925," and in the fall of the following year the likeness showed up on the back of the jacket of *The Sun Also Rises*.

Hemingway seems to have disliked this portrait of himself, though, and soon after seeing it on the jacket of his first novel, he groused about it to Max Perkins, his editor at Charles Scribner's Sons. Alluding to the journalist hero in *The Sun Also Rises*, Jake Barnes, who suffers from permanent impotence resulting from a wartime injury, Hemingway remarked that "the portrait . . . looks very much like a writer who had been saddened by the loss or atrophy of certain non replaceable parts. It is a pity it couldn't have been Barnes instead of Hemingway."[7] But as the owner of this portrait, Hemingway could presumably control its reproduction, and if he disliked it so much, why then had he released it for use on the jacket? That question is impossible to answer with certainty. Maybe he did not in fact dislike the portrait,

4
Hemingway likeness that appeared on the jacket of
The Sun Also Rises
John Blomshield
(circa 1895–after 1940),
pencil on paper, 22.2 x 19.2 cm
(8¾ x 11½ in.), 1925.
Ernest Hemingway Collection,
John F. Kennedy Library, Boston,
Massachusetts

and his unflattering take on it in his letter to Perkins was just a bit of self-deprecating humor. But funny cracks at his own expense were never a Hemingway specialty. More likely, his post-publication objection to the likeness was a manifestation of the postpartum gloom, irritability, and angst that Hemingway experienced in one degree or another after the completion of all of his major books.

In the early morning hours of March 4, 1928, Hemingway went into the bathroom of the Paris apartment he shared with his second wife, Pauline, only to find that someone had pulled the cord of the skylight and cracked the glass in the process. When he tried to correct the situation, the skylight came crashing down, cutting him severely on the forehead. Soon, blood running profusely down his face, he was being rushed to a hospital, where the wound was closed with nine stitches.

The accident was a freakish misfortune, but it also may have been something of a blessing. No sooner had the skylight fallen on Hemingway's head than his creative juices began churning. Within days, the new novel with which he had been struggling, about a professional revolutionist and his son, was forever put aside, and he was happily at work on a tale drawing on his experiences as an ambulance driver on the Italian front during World War I. Originally conceived as a short story, it quickly grew into a novel, and within six months the first draft was done. Its title was *A Farewell to Arms*, and it is considered by many to be the finest book Hemingway ever produced.

But preoccupied as he was with the beginnings of this new work, Hemingway was not too busy to do something about a pressing need at his publishers, Charles Scribner's Sons— some fresh pictures of him for publicity purposes. Early the previous November, Perkins had written him, "Pictures we do need badly. We have tried to have drawings made from photographs, but they are no good, and all the photographs have been used many times."[8] Hemingway had several times promised to get some pictures off to Perkins, but if he did, they were apparently unsatisfactory. Now, some four months later, he realized that he could simultaneously fill Scribner's photography needs and do a favor for an old friend of his ex-wife Hadley.

Helen Pierce Breaker had been a bridesmaid at Ernest and Hadley's wedding in 1921, and her husband George had given Hadley away. George had also been entrusted in 1924 with reinvesting a substantial portion of Hadley's modest trust funds. Instead, he had embezzled most of the money, while also embezzling funds from the bank that employed him. At some point in this story of malfeasance, Helen Breaker sued for divorce, and as her larcenous spouse was skipping to South America, she was preparing to go to Paris, where she hoped to parlay her amateur's interest in photography into a viable business specializing in portraiture.[9]

Fulfilling that ambition in a city like Paris, however, was not easy, and to get her start, Breaker needed more than just a camera and a studio. She also needed a prestigious client or two, whose likenesses might be easy to sell to publications and serve as a testament to her capabilities. Fortunately, the answer to that need was close at hand in the form of Hemingway, and in March 1928, the skylight wound still fresh on his forehead and the embryonic *A Farewell to Arms* taking shape in his mind, he obligingly sat before Breaker's camera.

Many of the photographs Breaker took at that session were little more than head-and-shoulder, coat-and-tie images of the more conventional sort. But when Hemingway shed his tie, opened his collar, doffed a dark sweater, and put on a visored cap for Breaker, she managed to produce some likenesses that went well beyond typical studio photograph portraiture (figure 5). Invested in them was a rough, masculine glamour that seemed to cast Hemingway

5
Images from the series of photographs taken by Helen Breaker in March 1928
Helen Breaker (circa 1895–circa 1939), gelatin silver prints, approximately 10.3 x 8.9 cm (4 ⅛ x 3 ½ in.), 1928. Ernest Hemingway Collection, John F. Kennedy Library, Boston, Massachusetts

6

Hemingway with Sylvia Beach in front of Shakespeare and Company
Unidentified photographer, gelatin silver print, 8.9 x 14 cm (3 ½ x 5 ½ in.), 1928. Sylvia Beach Collection, Department of Rare Books and Special Collections, Princeton University Library, Princeton, New Jersey

as the literary world's answer to a matinee idol. As Dorothy Parker put it, alluding to one of these pictures that ran in *Vanity Fair* in September 1928 and six months later in *Scribner's Monthly*, the image made "young women . . . all of a quiver" for information about him. "'Ooh,'" they said, according to Parker, "'do you know him? Ooh, I'd just *love* to meet him. Ooh, tell me what he's like.'" Parker found the image so captivating that she wondered whether its publication "was perhaps a mistake," apparently because it drew too much attention away from Hemingway's virtues as a writer.[10]

But while Breaker's Hemingway may have set some hearts aflutter, it is not altogether clear just how much of the hoped-for boost the picture provided to her nascent career. She did, however, ultimately succeed in establishing a modestly successful photography studio in Paris and eventually won admission to the Académie de photographie française. Unfortunately, in the 1930s her eyesight began to deteriorate sharply, and on the eve of World War II, she committed suicide.

On March 17, 1928, shortly after posing for Helen Breaker's photographs, Hemingway boarded a ship headed for Cuba. He planned to continue to Key West, where he intended to combine writing with some deep-sea fishing. With him was Pauline, whom he had married the previous year, soon after his divorce from Hadley. His period of residence in Paris was for the most part over, and he would eventually come to regard Key West as his home base. But before he left to catch his boat at La Rochelle, there was one more significant image from his Paris years to be made. This time it was not a painted likeness or a posed studio photograph. It was instead a snapshot (figure 6). The occasion was a little celebration at Shakespeare and Company of Sylvia Beach's forty-first birthday, March 14, and it showed Hemingway and Beach standing in front of the shop. With them were Myrsine Moschos, a longtime clerk in the shop, and her mildly retarded sister Hélène, who regularly ran errands for Beach. There is nothing distinguished about the composition of the picture, and there is no record of who took it. It is simply a lineup of smiling people, typical of the kind seen in amateur snapshots taken at thousands of social gatherings. Despite its ordinariness, it occupies an important spot in the Hemingway iconography. For in the pictorial archive documenting the group of American writers who came to Paris in the 1920s to further their art, this anonymously made picture ranks easily among the most frequently reproduced. For all its haphazard informality—Hemingway lazily supporting himself against the shop's door, his wounded head wrapped, and Beach looking away from the camera—it has thus become an emblematic evocation of a noteworthy time and place in American letters.

After arriving in Key West in April 1928, Hemingway quickly fell into a routine. Generally rising early, he spent his mornings working on A Farewell to Arms. Afternoons were given over to fishing and getting to know some of the local citizenry. Making good progress on his novel and learning the tricks of saltwater fishing, he was enjoying himself immensely, and he was soon urging some of his cronies to come join him in the good life.

Among those succumbing to his urgings was the painter Waldo Peirce. A Harvard graduate and member of a Maine family that had made a fortune in lumbering, Peirce had spent much time in the 1920s studying and working in Europe. The big, bearded Peirce was a fun-loving character whose antics became the basis of oft-repeated tales. In one, he jumped off a Europe-bound ship into Boston Harbor, leaving his Harvard classmate John Reed on board to face charges of murdering his vanished traveling companion. With his Rabelaisian humor and his taste for carousing, he fit splendidly the Hemingway definition of a boon companion, and from the moment they met in Paris in the spring of 1927, the two were fast friends.[11]

Peirce may have been invited to Key West because Hemingway liked his company. But his several extended visits there in the late 1920s and early 1930s produced more than good times. They also yielded a substantial contribution to the fund of Hemingway imagery.

Peirce's first attempt at recording Hemingway's features, in May 1928, was prompted by Max Perkins, who had been a classmate of Peirce's twenty years earlier. On hearing that the artist would soon be joining Hemingway in Key West for a month or so, he asked Hemingway to see what he could do to "make Waldo try his hand at something with an eye to publication."[12] The convivial Peirce was happy to oblige, and two surviving ink drawings of Hemingway by him date from that spring in Key West. When Peirce showed up shortly thereafter at Perkins's office with the more finished of the two (figure 7), showing the writer in an authorly, contemplative pose, Perkins was thrilled, and he told Hemingway, "We are going to use it right away."[13] Not long afterward, the image was running in *Brentano's Book Chats* with an article by Malcolm Cowley entitled "The Hemingway Legend." In fall 1929 the *Saturday Review of Literature* carried it in tandem with a review of *A Farewell to Arms*, which declared, among other things, that "you cannot take too seriously a novel of such vivid reality," nor an author of "such uncanny powers."[14]

Peirce's stint as a Hemingway portraitist had only begun. During his next stay in Key West, in February–March 1929, he completed another likeness, this time in oil (figure 8). At first glance, the portrait seems to have fallen a step short of capturing a good, characteristic sense of the writer, and it engenders momentary suspicions that it is the likeness of someone trying to look like Hemingway. In fact, it is quite the reverse, and to appreciate the picture fully, it is necessary to go back to Max Perkins's report in a letter to Hemingway that the editor's friend Mary Colum, herself a writer and literary critic, "says you look like Balzac."[15]

Given the jowly corpulence evident in so many images of Honoré de Balzac, Hemingway might have taken offense at this physical comparison to the French writer. But apparently he

7
Waldo Peirce's first portrait of Hemingway
Waldo Peirce (1884–1970), pen and ink on paper, 50.8 x 38.1 cm (20 x 15 in.), 1928. National Portrait Gallery, Smithsonian Institution, Washington, D.C.; gift of Jonathan Peirce

found this link to the man who had been such a salient figure in the shift from romanticism to realism in Western fiction rather appealing, and Colum's remark stuck in his mind. As a result, when Peirce set up his easel to begin another group of sittings with Hemingway in the winter of 1929, the subject's instruction to his portraitist seems to have been something akin to "Why don't you try to make me look like Balzac this time?" It is equally easy to imagine Peirce, good-humored soul that he was, enthusiastically joining into the spirit of this proposed conceit, and as he set brush to canvas, no doubt one of the visual references close at hand was a variant of the many printed Balzac likenesses made from a daguerreotype taken in the late 1840s (figure 9).

Peirce did not, however, do anything so obvious as superimposing Hemingway's facial features on a line-for-line replication of the Balzac likeness. His borrowing from that image was far more subtle, and the resulting portrait was decidedly more Hemingway than Balzac and more twentieth century than nineteenth century. Still, the Balzac presence was there, and lest anyone miss it, before Peirce presented the picture to Hemingway on its completion, he inscribed it "for Ernest / (alias Kid Balzac)."

In theatrical portraiture, there is a long tradition of actors and actresses portrayed in roles that they made famous. The impulse to want a memento of that sort is understandable. But why should Hemingway want to be depicted in the guise of another writer? To some

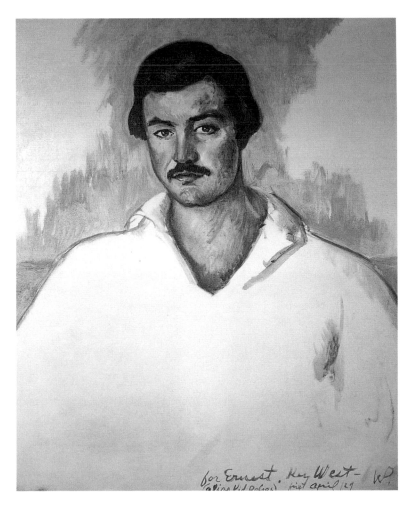

9
Image made from a daguerreotype of Honoré de Balzac
Prints and Photographs Division, Library of Congress, Washington, D.C.

8
Hemingway as "Kid Balzac"
Waldo Peirce (1884–1970), oil on canvas, 78.7 x 62.8 cm (31 x 24 ¾ in.), 1929. Ernest Hemingway Collection, John F. Kennedy Library, Boston, Massachusetts

10
Death in the Gulf Stream,
**Hemingway and company bearding
a shark near Key West**
Waldo Peirce (1884–1970), oil on canvas,
63.5 x 81.2 cm (25 x 32 in.), 1932.
Michael Peirce

extent, it may simply have been a reflection of his love for the double-entendre insider's joke
that had manifested itself to such good effect in the bantering dialogue of *The Sun Also Rises*.
But it was likely also an expression of Hemingway's competitive instinct, which was unrelenting, and could sometimes surface in unseemly ways. When it came to writing, that com-
petitiveness took the form of a frequent need to measure himself against other writers and,
on one occasion, even to discuss his literary triumphs as if they were boxing matches where
he had bested the likes of the Russian novelist Ivan Turgenev or the French short story
writer Guy de Maupassant. In other words, for Hemingway, who had just sent off the final
draft of *A Farewell to Arms* to Scribner and was feeling pretty good about it, being cast as a
modern-day Balzac may have been a means of scoring where he stood in the current literary
competition.[16]

"Alias Kid Balzac" was not the last of Peirce's efforts to paint his friend Hemingway.
Though a serious artist, Peirce was also an inveterate composer of funny pictures on the side.
Most often his comic pictures took the form of quick ink and watercolor sketches. But sometimes they became quite formidable, and in 1932 he immortalized his Key West fishing adventures with Hemingway in a farcical oil painting titled *Death in the Gulf Stream* (figure 10). In
the work, Peirce himself tranquilly sits in the stern of a small boat, guiding it with a pole; in
the bow stands another Hemingway fishing pal, his boyhood friend Bill Smith, tugging
mightily on a rope attached to a harpoon, which is stuck in turn in the body of a leaping
shark; at the center of the composition is a gun-wielding Hemingway, who puts an end to the
shark by shooting into its underside.

There is a Three Stooges desperation about this scene, owing largely to a sense that these
three sportsmen do not really know what they are about and are perhaps too dim to under-

stand their peril in taking on such a large, deadly fish in their small boat. The picture's slap-stick quality also leaves the viewer with the feeling that it must depict a purely fictional event, at most one inspired by the fishing high jinks of the three protagonists in it. In fact, a collection of photographs, taken with Peirce's camera and sent to Shakespeare and Company for the entertainment of Sylvia Beach, shows that a tussle with a shark along these very lines did indeed occur during Peirce's first Key West visit with Hemingway in 1928.[17] Thus Peirce not only commemorated here the beginnings of Hemingway's rise as one of the world's most famous salt-water fishermen; in his own zany fashion, he documented it as well.

That picture was made for Peirce's private pleasure and the amusement of his friends. On the other hand, his final likeness of Hemingway was made for decidedly public consumption. The occasion was the publication in 1937 of Hemingway's *To Have and Have Not*, his first novel since *A Farewell to Arms*, published eight years earlier. To mark the event, *Time* magazine featured the writer on its cover and commissioned Peirce to produce the image. Based on a snapshot found among the same group of Peirce photographs recording the shark incident, the finished picture was not an especially good likeness (figure 11). Nor was it the sort of image one normally associates with serious writers. Nevertheless, it was an apt reflection of a noteworthy transformation the Hemingway persona had undergone in the popular imagination in the past five or six years.

Aside from a number of distinguished short stories, Hemingway had produced nothing in that period to advance his reputation as a fiction writer, and there were those who had begun to wonder whether his once shimmering light as a novelist had spent its fuel. Meanwhile, however, thanks to widely circulated news items and pictures on his fishing exploits in Key West, his own writing on those exploits for *Esquire* magazine, and his articles and book on his big-game safari to Africa in 1933–1934, his celebrity as a virile, suntanned sportsman of considerable prowess had taken a quantum leap. A book on deep-sea fishing in 1936 went so far as to rate him one of the two greatest fishermen in the world. The contemplative man of letters had, in short, become the man of action, and Peirce's *Time* cover portrait, showing him straining to reel in some big, unseen fish, was by now just what the public had come to expect of a Hemingway likeness.

Not everyone was particularly taken with Hemingway's virile public image, and as his writings and lifestyle began giving it shape in the early 1930s, a school of Hemingway observers emerged who found the mounting testaments to his tough masculinity absurdly excessive and a bit tiresome. Among the members of that school was writer Max Eastman, who gave voice to his feelings in June 1933 in a review for the *New Republic* of Hemingway's recently published book on the art of bullfighting, *Death in the Afternoon*. A work born of a passion that had its beginnings in the summer of 1923, when Hemingway witnessed his first bullfight, the volume teemed with evidences of reverence for this ancient blood sport as a quintessential test of masculine virtue and courage. Eastman, however, did not share that reverence and dismissed it all as "rather sophomoric." Moreover, the impetus for the book, he speculated, stemmed from Hemingway's lack of "the serene confidence that he is a full-sized man," which led in turn to "a continual sense of obligation to put forth evidences of

FIFTEEN CENTS

October 18, 1937

TIME

The Weekly Newsmagazine

(See BOOKS)

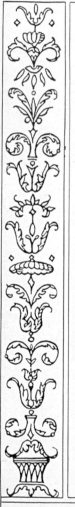

Waldo Peirce

ERNEST MILLER HEMINGWAY

Volume XXX

"A man ain't got no hasn't got any can't really isn't any way out."
(See BOOKS)

Number 16

red-blooded masculinity." And among the more unfortunate fruits of that was the growing currency in some quarters of "a literary style, you might say, of wearing false hair on the chest."[18]

Hemingway would have been wise to let Eastman's observations go unanswered. But he was constitutionally incapable of that. Interpreting Eastman's words as a public accusation of sexual impotence, he instead turned the matter into an irresistibly zesty morsel for the publishing world gossip mill. After wiring Max Perkins to "Tell your friend Eastman [I] will break his jaw," he fired off a letter to the *New Republic*, sarcastically asking Eastman to "elaborate his nostalgic speculations on my sexual incapacity" and assuring the magazine that "here they would be read (aloud) with much enjoyment."[19] To clear the air, *New Republic* was soon running a letter from Eastman explaining that, when considered in the full context of his piece on *Death in the Afternoon*, the allegation that he meant to question Hemingway's manhood was groundless. But even that did not satisfy, and the incident did not play itself out until 1937, in a ludicrous scene in Max Perkins's office, where Hemingway and Eastman ended up actually comparing the hair on their respective chests and then wrestling each other to the floor.

While Hemingway fumed, others were mightily amused. Not least of them was Miguel Covarrubias, a Mexican-born caricaturist who, following his arrival in New York in the early 1920s, quickly carved out a reputation as one of the most wickedly funny pictorial satirists of the day. Covarrubias was a regular contributor to the pages of *Vanity Fair*, and among his most memorable works was his "Impossible Interview" series for that magazine, featuring friendly chats between such figures as notorious mobster Al Capone and United States Chief Justice Charles Evans Hughes.[20] In summer 1933 the artist was contemplating yet another series for *Vanity Fair*, "Private Lives of the Great." Here the intention was to depict current notables engaged in imagined private pastimes they would just as soon not have their admiring publics know about, and it was for the "Private Lives" series that Covarrubias conceived a wonderfully witty commentary that took its cue directly from the Hemingway-Eastman spat (figure 12). In it, he transformed Hemingway into a leopard-skin-clad Tarzan trying to replace the false chest hair that Eastman had accused him of sporting in his books by massaging himself with a hair-sprouting elixir.

Humor at his own expense was never Hemingway's long suit, and Covarrubias's pictorial play on Eastman's observations about his writing would have made him bristle. As it turned out, however, he never had a chance to get angry. The staff of *Vanity Fair* deemed the bare-chested caricature "a bit on the questionable side as far as taste is concerned," and the magazine, much to the artist's chagrin, never ran it.[21] In an irony worthy of a short story, Hemingway was saved from any embarrassment the image's publication might cause him by the Victorian outlook he so deplored when it prompted his publisher to tone down the raciness and profanity in his own work.

Published or not, the image stands as one of the most entertaining evocations of Hemingway's growing reputation in the 1930s as the he-man of American letters, and it is instructive to consider Covarrubias's caricature in tandem with the critic Clifton Fadiman's reflections on the contemporary state of Hemingway's public persona for *The Nation* in 1933,

11
Peirce's portrait of Hemingway on the cover of *Time,* October 18, 1937
Time magazine. Copyright © Time, Inc.

where Fadiman, among other things, dubbed him "the frontiersman of the loins, heart, and biceps."[22]

About the time that Covarrubias was dreaming up his Tarzanlike lampoon, Hemingway was preparing for a venture that would yield a he-man image of a sort much more to his liking. The venue was East Africa, and the venture in question was a hunting safari, which he had been planning for several years. After several delays, he finally began it in late December 1933. Hemingway had brought along a Graphlex camera and lots of film for the occasion, and among the pictures snapped in the course of his two-month trek through the game-filled plains and valleys of Kenya and present-day Tanzania was one of Hemingway kneeling in the grass before the spiraled horns of two greater kudus (figure 13). Taken on one of the last days of the safari, the picture shows him handsomely aglow with pride as he grasps these two trophies. Of the scores of surviving photographs of Hemingway posed with prizes from his fishing and hunting expeditions, it is easily one of the most striking.

But it is not just a good photograph; it is also a visual epigraph to a phase of the safari that was to become the inspiration for a literary experiment, *The Green Hills of Africa*, Hemingway's self-confessed attempt to enlist the forms of novel fiction to tell the factual story of his quest for the kudu.

12

Miguel Covarrubias's portrayal of Hemingway the he-man
Miguel Covarrubias (1902–57), gouache on board, 30.5 x 25.4 cm (12 x 10 in.), 1933. Prints and Photographs Division, Library of Congress, Washington, D.C.

13
Hemingway with the horns of his kudus and an oryx
Unidentified photographer, gelatin silver print, 24.1 x 30.4 cm (9 ½ x 12 in.), 1934.
Ernest Hemingway Collection, John F. Kennedy Library, Boston, Massachusetts

In spite of a severe bout of amoebic dysentery that had required hospitalization in Nairobi, Hemingway had managed to bag an impressive list of African game well before the safari was to end in mid-February 1934. Among his trophies were a lion, a buffalo, a cheetah, a leopard, and a rhinoceros. For both him and his hunting companion, Key West friend Charles Thompson, though, the magnificently horned kudu remained frustratingly elusive. Finally Thompson downed one. But to the chagrin of the intensely competitive Hemingway, who was already nettled by the fact that Thompson's game trophies were consistently larger than his own, the kudu remained out of his line of fire. Then, late one afternoon, just as the onset of the rainy season was about to force an end to the safari, he and his gun bearer and trackers spotted kudus in the distance. Taking aim, he shot not one but two of them. Better yet, Hemingway was elated to find that one of them was substantially larger than the kudu Thompson had bagged.

Unfortunately, the elation on that count was short-lived. Upon driving into the safari's base camp, the horns of his kudus magnificently "curling out the back of the car," Hemingway learned that while he had been out stalking his own kudu, Thompson had himself shot another. Comparison of the horns indicated that of the safari party's four downed kudus, Thompson's second was easily the most formidable. By his own admission, Hemingway was suddenly "poisoned with envy," and he had all he could do to congratulate Thompson for once again besting him.[23] But the sourness did not hang on. By the time he came to pose grinningly with the horns of his two kudus, he was clearly in better spirits. Maybe it was because he knew that he had the makings of another book.

According to the critics, at least, 1937 was not an especially good time for Hemingway. *To Have and Have Not* appeared that fall to poor reviews. One critic suggested that Hemingway's literary reputation would have been stronger "if it had never been published," while another observed that the book lacked "unity and sureness of effect." Echoing that opinion, a third reviewer remarked on "an unusual clumsiness" in the narrative, which he took as a sign that Hemingway was "rather less sure of himself than usual."[24]

In terms of celebrity, however, 1937 yielded Hemingway a fine vintage. Late in 1936 the North American Newspaper Alliance had agreed to pay him one dollar a word to cover the Spanish civil war, which had broken out the previous summer. It was exceptionally good money, said at the time to be the highest rate ever paid a war correspondent. Besides, Hemingway loved Spain, and he had a strong desire to see firsthand how the republican Loyalists, whose cause he supported, were faring against the rebel fascists led by Francisco Franco. The deal was impossible to resist, and in early March 1937, *Newsweek* reported that Hemingway had sailed for Spain, in the words of the writer himself, to "'make money the hard way, as a working newspaper correspondent.'"[25]

The puffing tone of that remark notwithstanding, Hemingway did in fact earn a good deal of his pay the hard way, and in the course of his three correspondent stints in 1937–38—each lasting several months—he took a good many risks to gather material for his dispatches in the front lines. He also did some creditable reporting. At the same time, however, he was adding a new dimension to his celebrity, for his dispatches did not just cover the war. They did a pretty good job of covering Hemingway as well, and his reporting—often cast in the first person singular—frequently placed the limelight as much on his courage in the line of fire and military expertise as it did on the civil war itself. As a result, newsman Hemingway became news in himself, and to the other ingredients of his public persona—innovative man of letters, bullfighting aficionado, outdoor sportsman—was now added brave and knowing war correspondent.

The most obvious evidence of that development was the way Hemingway's coverage of the war became a sort of substory of the conflict in the press. At his departures for Spain and his returns, for example, the press was there to interview him, and in both *Newsweek* and *Time* there was even a progress report on the war, which almost seemed a mere pretext to talk about Hemingway.[26]

Also testifying to Hemingway's new source of fame was a series of photographs made at the time of the battle of Teruel in late 1937 by Robert Capa. Born Endre (later André) Freidmann in Hungary, Capa had been catapulted to a fame of his own with his pictures of the Spanish civil war. The most noteworthy of them by far was his dramatic photograph of a dying Loyalist soldier taken on a Spanish hillside. A much-reproduced classic in the annals of twentieth-century war imagery, the picture captured its subject just as the fatal bullet struck, and with its publication in September 1936, Capa began his rise as one of the foremost war photographers of his time.

Capa first met Hemingway in spring 1937 in Madrid. Although few particulars of that encounter are known, it can be assumed that it was a symbiotic relationship from the outset. Capa's bon vivant ways and earthy good humor were exactly the traits that Hemingway liked in his companions, and Capa later observed that he "adopted [the writer] as a father"—an act that could only cement their comradeship further, given Hemingway's relish for the paternal role in his personal relationships.[27] But Capa saw in Hemingway a promising commercial opportunity as well. When the two met again at the battle for the town of Teruel in December 1937, he decided to make Hemingway the focus of a group of pictures that could be marketed to some European or American publication as a photo story.

The series began with shots of Hemingway in his hotel room in Valencia, preparing to go to the Teruel front by familiarizing himself with the terrain via maps. Then it was on to the front itself, where Capa photographed him in a tattered tweed jacket seeking respite from the brutal pre-Christmas cold at a fire, talking to Loyalist soldiers (figure 14), and looking at a tattered book under a bright winter sun (figure 15). The most engaging of them depicted him sprawled in the tall grass, partially protected from enemy fire by the gentle slope of the land, showing a young Loyalist soldier how to unjam his rifle with a rock (figure 16).

Unfortunately, Capa never found a taker for his Hemingway picture story. He did manage, however, to place some of the photographs individually with various publications. Among the published images was one that ran in *Life* early in 1940, showing the writer about to down a prebreakfast swig of Scotch from a bottle to brace himself against the cold (figure 17). "In Spain's sub-zero winter," the magazine noted in the caption, "he sometimes had to

14
Hemingway talking with a Loyalist soldier during the battle for Teruel
Robert Capa (1913–54), gelatin silver print, 16.5 x 23.2 cm (6 ½ x 9 ⅛ in.), 1937. Ernest Hemingway Collection, John F. Kennedy Library, Boston, Massachusetts. Copyright © Robert Capa Archives, ICP

15
Hemingway examining his notes at the battle for Teruel
Robert Capa (1913–54), gelatin silver print, 22.9 x 17.1 cm (9 x 6 ¾ in.), 1937. Ernest Hemingway Collection, John F. Kennedy Library, Boston, Massachusetts. Copyright © Robert Capa Archives, ICP

16
**Hemingway helping a soldier
unjam his rifle at the battle for Teruel**
Robert Capa (1913–54), gelatin silver
print, 17.4 x 24.1 cm (6⅞ x 9½ in.), 1937.
Ernest Hemingway Collection,
John F. Kennedy Library, Boston,
Massachusetts. Copyright ©
Robert Capa Archives, ICP

17
**Hemingway taking a swig of Scotch
in hotel room during battle for Teruel**
Robert Capa (1913–54), photograph, 1937.
Courtesy Magnum Photos, Inc., New
York City. Copyright © Robert Capa
Archives, ICP

wash his face with whiskey."[28] The picture seems artificially posed, especially in the way Hemingway holds the bottle to his mouth. Hokey or not, it doubtless helped to fix Hemingway's new reputation as toughened war correspondent in the popular imagination.

The Teruel pictures, however, are not simply testimony to transitory image making. They are also mementos of a prelude to one of the most lasting of Hemingway's literary achievements. Shortly after getting back to Key West, he wrote to Max Perkins that "Teruel was the best thing I've ever had I think."[29] Precisely what that joyous outburst meant is difficult to say, but Hemingway likely felt that Teruel, and the excitement of covering the civil war in general, had primed his creative juices. Although the short story based on the Teruel experience that he had hoped to do went forever unwritten, a far more important piece about the civil war was now taking shape in his mind. Its title would be *For Whom the Bell Tolls*, and its popular and critical success would discredit that school of thought that Hemingway's greatest achievements in fiction were well behind him.

Hemingway had enjoyed being witness to the Spanish civil war far too much to forgo a chance to be a player in World War II. When the United States entered into that conflict in late 1941, it was inevitable that he should find a way to be actively involved. Hemingway was residing in Cuba with his third wife, Martha Gellhorn, and for awhile he satisfied his guns-and-drums craving by running a clandestine operation, in league with some of his local friends and under American embassy auspices, that sought to ferret out German spies operating in Havana. Dubbed the Crook Factory, the group came up with some useful information, according to the U.S. ambassador. But by late fall 1942, Hemingway had removed himself from the operation and was launching yet another war-related venture. Arming his boat with grenades and machine guns, he and some of his acquaintances began patrolling the waters around Cuba for German submarines that were posing a threat to vital Allied shipping. This reconnaissance effort, which lasted several months, yielded little solid information about submarine whereabouts, and it certainly produced no chance encounter with a surfaced U-boat that would allow Hemingway and his crew to implement their plan to disable it by lobbing explosives into its conning tower or down its hatches.

Hemingway's wife did not think much of his ventures into intelligence and submarine spotting. With prodding from Martha, he finally decided to get closer to the war, and in spring 1944 he agreed to cover it for *Collier's* magazine. By late May he was settling into the Dorchester Hotel in London just as the Allies were preparing to launch the biggest military action in history, the invasion of Normandy.

His literary fame alone guaranteed that Hemingway would cut a substantial figure in the Allied press corps. But also feeding his notoriety on the battlefields of northern France, and later Germany, was his irrepressible drive to be more than a mere correspondent. Simply put, Hemingway wanted to be a soldier. And no silly Geneva Convention forbidding frontline reporters from bearing arms or participating in military action was going to deny him that opportunity. By early August, he was claiming that he had killed six Germans with a hand grenade lobbed into a French cellar. His soldiering really got serious, however, about three weeks later at the town of Rambouillet, about twenty-five miles southwest of Paris. There, linking up with French resistance fighters who obligingly took to calling him "le grand capi-taine" and "colonel," he promptly began using his army connections to procure arms for "his men" and to turn his hotel room into an arsenal abrim with guns and ammunition. He was also launching reconnaissance operations to pinpoint remaining pockets of German resistance between Rambouillet and Paris.

Amidst his Rambouillet adventures and later incidents, in which he crossed the line from observer to combatant, Hemingway was having the time of his life. Meanwhile, there were two schools of thought emerging about his wartime behavior. On the one hand, there were those who heartily disapproved his flouting of the Geneva Convention, some of whom prompted an official investigation into it. Allied to these anti-Hemingwayites were others who found the hairy-chested posturings that came with his soldierly pursuits decidedly silly and childish. At the other end of the scale were those who could not resist the Hemingway bonhomie and charisma and admired him unreservedly. Not least of his fans was Colonel Charles Lanham, with whose regiment Hemingway spent much time. Recalling the spell the writer wove over him at a dinner near the German border in fall 1944, Lanham noted: "We all seemed for the moment like minor gods, and Hemingway, presiding at the head of the table, might have been a fatherly Mars delighting in the happiness of his brood."[30]

Another who succumbed to the Hemingway magic was the correspondent artist John Groth, who met him in late September 1944 along Germany's recently penetrated defenses known as the Siegfried Line. Liking nothing more during his childhood than to wile away his time drawing depictions of war, Groth had come to the European theater for the Chicago Sun Syndicate. When he first encountered Hemingway at the latter's quarters in a commandeered German farmhouse, he was bowled over at coming face to face with this great man of letters. "I couldn't open my mouth," he noted later, and "sat there like a country bumpkin."

Hemingway put him at his ease, offering him some cognac and insisting that he stay at the farmhouse for a while. Then they sat down to share a meal, where Hemingway dominated the conversation with a stream of war stories. Groth was in seventh heaven hearing such anecdotes from "the master storyteller himself." But he was not so euphoric that he lacked the presence of mind to record the moment for posterity. At the meal's end he pulled out the tools of his trade to make a drawing or two.

One sketch Groth made during their shared residence at the front lines showed Hemingway seated at a table with what appears to be a grenade strapped to his shoulder, in violation of the Geneva convention (figure 18). Milling around him are some of the many soldiers who gravitated to his quarters for talk, refreshments, and autographs. The picture is not an especially good likeness. Nevertheless, Hemingway's looming centrality in the composition makes it a rather striking evocation of his magnetic wartime presence, at least as it made itself felt to Groth. Remembering their time together a few years later, the artist noted: "Hemingway was huge even when seated, flanked by GIs. The eye stayed on him as on the central figure of 'The Last Supper.'" Later in that same recollection, Groth noted that when Hemingway left the front to return to Paris, his absence left a huge vacuum. The place now seemed "like a French town that had lost its cathedral."[31]

18
Drawing of Hemingway in German farmhouse near the Siegfried Line
John Groth (1908–88), ink and wash, 76.2 x 101.5 cm (30 x 40 in.), 1944. Art Collection, Harry Ransom Humanities Research Center, The University of Texas at Austin

Hemingway's return from the war to his home in Cuba in early 1945 coincided with yet another major change in his marital life. With his marriage to Martha Gellhorn already on shaky ground, he had met Time-Life staffer Mary Welsh during his stay in Europe, fallen in love, and ultimately proposed marriage. Now all that remained was to wait until the couple's divorces from their respective spouses came through.

The homecoming also ushered in the final phase of Hemingway's career. In quantitative terms, his literary productivity was prodigious in this period, including three novels, two of which would be published posthumously, and a memoir of his Paris years that also appeared after his death. But in the sixteen years that remained to him, he produced only one work, his novella *The Old Man and the Sea*, that approached the critical stature of *A Farewell to Arms*, *The Sun Also Rises*, or some of his earlier short stories. Nevertheless, this was a time of important honors. In 1953, the best-selling *Old Man and the Sea* earned him a Pulitzer Prize—an award that had been denied *For Whom the Bell Tolls* because its love scenes were deemed too racy. In spring 1954 the American Academy of Arts and Letters presented him with its Award of Merit. Finally, in the same year, he claimed that most rarefied form of recognition, the Nobel Prize in literature, given in honor of his "style-making mastery of the art of modern narrative."[32]

But there was yet another kind of honor, which did not involve medals and citations, falling to Hemingway in the last decade and a half of his life. Between critical admiration for his original artistry and his glamorous reputation, he had become by the 1950s a celebrity of the first rank. To the public at large, many of whom had never read his work, his face was as familiar as a movie star's; at a place like New York's Stork Club, it was hard to say whose patronage most enhanced its reputation as a celebrity hangout—Hemingway's or that of someone like Ingrid Bergman. As one Hemingway scholar put it: "He once made news because of what he did; now he made news because of who he was."[33]

Undoubtedly one of the most convincing substantiations of that observation occurred in 1953, when the writer and his wife, Mary, went on a hunting safari to eastern Africa. The previous year, *Life* had staged a coup that was the envy of its picture-magazine competitors: with a dramatically close-cropped black-and-white photograph portrait of Hemingway on its cover and another in full color featured inside, it had run *The Old Man and the Sea* in its entirety. For this prepublication privilege, the magazine had paid Hemingway the handsome sum of $40,000, and the result had been well worth the fee. Within forty-eight hours of reaching the newsstands, *Life*'s *Old Man and the Sea* issue of more than 5.3 million was sold out. If proof were needed that Hemingway made good circulation-boosting copy, this was surely it, and when he began contemplating his trip to Africa, *Life*'s competitor, *Look*, wasted no time in trying to enlist the Hemingway magic on behalf of its own circulation. According to the terms offered, the magazine would defray $15,000 of the expense for Hemingway's African sojourn if it could send a photographer with him to do a picture story, and it would throw in $10,000 more if Hemingway himself would supply 3,500 words worth of hunting anecdotes to accompany the pictures.

It was a deal impossible to refuse, and accompanying the Hemingway party when it set out on its safari on September 1, 1953, was *Look* photographer Earl Theisen. A low-key, easygoing sort, Theisen blended in well with the party, which included an entourage of some twenty-two native servants. Writing Hemingway several months after leaving the safari to return to the United States, he fondly described the experience as "by far my 'best ever' trip."[34]

Even so, the assignment had its frustrations. Due in large part to heavy drinking, Hemingway was having trouble living up to his heroic hunter's image. As a result, Theisen became irritated that he was not getting the pictures he had expected. Ultimately, however, he came up with a photograph that made the whole venture worthwhile for all concerned (figure 19). It was, according to Mary Hemingway's account, October 1. Hemingway was hunting in the company of Mary and Mayito Menocal, a Cuban friend. They were climbing a hill with their gun bearers when Menocal spotted a leopard and started shooting. Quickly Hemingway took aim at the animal as well, and within seconds the leopard lay dead some twenty paces away. The event was, as Mary put it, "a gift from On High for Earl Theisen," and soon the photographer was focusing his camera on a faintly beaming Hemingway, seated on the ground next to the leopard lying in the foreground.[35] The pictures that came out of this photography session were enough to warm the heart of a Hollywood publicist. Here, with his serenely gray-bearded countenance and his rifle at the ready, was an elder statesman of letters tailor-made for popular American taste—sage enough to affirm his intellectual worthiness, yet rugged enough to appeal to Americans' long-standing weakness for the man of action and derring-do.

Engaging as these images were, there was one thing wrong with them. They all implied that the leopard was Hemingway's kill when, in fact, it was not at all certain who had felled the animal—he or his friend Menocal. Hemingway himself did not consider this a point worth bothering about. But Mary did, and she declared it a matter of "moral disintegration" to think of publishing one of the photographs in *Look*.[36] According to Mary, Hemingway was not inclined to buy that argument. Nevertheless, he finally gave a grudging promise that no picture from this series of images would be published unless he truly did get a leopard that was unambiguously his own. Fortunately for all concerned, particularly *Look*, he did. In its sixteen-page spread on the Hemingway safari, the leopard photograph was clearly the standout, and without it, the magazine might not have been altogether sure that it had gotten its money's worth.

Following its maiden appearance in *Look*, Theisen received many requests for the leopard photograph, but he was reluctant to let it out for reasons that are not entirely clear. Judging from correspondence with Hemingway, it seems that he was afraid of its becoming stale before it could be featured in a projected book on his own work and in a book on the safari that Hemingway was thinking about writing.[37] Unfortunately, Theisen's volume never materialized, and it was more than forty-five years before Hemingway's safari account took book form.

While Theisen kept his *Hemingway* under wraps, there was another photograph of the writer in the offing that was equally striking, and its maker had no qualms whatsoever about letting it out. The photographer in question was the Armenian-born Yousuf Karsh, who first made his mark as the portraitist of world luminaries with his photograph of Winston Churchill in 1941. Karsh made his likeness of Hemingway in Cuba in March 1957, and at the outset, his client for this commission was *Life*, which hoped to use it with an autobiographical article that it wanted Hemingway to write.

When Karsh arrived in Cuba, Hemingway was struggling with an accumulation of assorted health problems. Early in 1954, while still on safari, he and Mary had lived through two small-plane crashes that left him with a litany of injuries, including a fractured skull and concussion, two cracked spinal discs, and damage to several internal organs. Recovery was not easy, and over the next two years he suffered from a host of other physical ailments, ranging from hepatitis, nephritis, and anemia to distressingly high blood pressure and cholesterol levels. Finally, to correct the latter two ailments, a doctor put him on a strict diet in late 1956 and ordered him to sharply curtail his heavy alcohol intake. Hemingway obeyed the regimen, but not gleefully, and the abstemious, calorie-counting writer was not exactly in buoyant spirits when he confronted Karsh's camera lens. In fact, so low-key was his manner that Karsh later described him as "the shyest man I ever photographed."[38]

19
Hemingway with dead leopard
Earl Theisen (1903–73), gelatin silver print, 23.1 x 18.4 cm (9 ⅛ x 7 ¼ in.), 1953. Ernest Hemingway Collection, John F. Kennedy Library, Boston, Massachusetts. Copyright © 1998 Earl Theisen Archives

Karsh was by no means the first to experience Hemingway's shyness with people he did not know well. Still, the author could muster an impressive presence. Moreover, Karsh was a master at enhancing it, and among the several images that came out of the Karsh sittings was one that was nothing short of leonine (figure 20). In this picture and a number of others from the sitting as well, Hemingway wore a heavy turtleneck sweater from a Christian Dior Paris boutique that Mary had given him the previous Christmas. It had been quite expensive, and Mary had felt quite extravagant when she purchased it.[39] But it was worth every penny. The sweater was an ideal foil for Hemingway's tanned, bearded features, and it was clearly one of the elements that invested the likeness with a quality that was downright biblical. More important, however, than how this Moseslike venerability was created was how it at once mirrored and fed a larger-than-life conception of Hemingway that had taken hold in the popular imagination.

Not surprisingly, the portrait proved eminently salable. Although the original impetus for the picture, an autobiographical article in *Life*, fell through, Karsh found any number of publications eager to publish it, including *Atlantic Monthly*, which ran with it the photographer's own account of the picture's circumstances. In the process, it became the all but official image of Hemingway in his later years. For Karsh, the picture's wide circulation also yielded an amusing sidelight—a marked upsurge in enthusiasm among his subjects for posing in sweaters.

While Karsh's sweatered portrait was staking its claim as the ultimate Hemingway icon, a much less heralded group of Hemingway photographs, by freelance photojournalist John Bryson, was in the making. Less heralded did not mean less noteworthy. Taken in late 1958 or early 1959, the Bryson photographs include some of the most interesting visual documents from the last years of the writer's life.

The irony of these pictures is that Bryson never expected to take them at all. At the time of his visit to the Hemingways, they were settled into a rented house in Ketchum, Idaho. They had moved there in fall 1958, in large part to get away from civil unrest in Cuba that was about to erupt into revolution and drive them permanently from their home near Havana. Bryson was on assignment for the syndicated Sunday supplement magazine *This Week*, and he had come to Ketchum to photograph not Ernest but Mary Hemingway. Over the years Mary had become a good cook and was particularly adept at preparing dishes from the fish and wild game that she and her husband caught. As a result, the magazine's food editor wanted to do a column featuring a favorite recipe from Mary's kitchen and a picture of her preparing it. At the outset, this looked like a routine assignment to Bryson. When he set out for Ketchum from his Los Angeles base, he anticipated spending no more than a day or so there.

What Bryson did not factor into that timetable was Hemingway's mood. After nearly two years of limiting his food and alcohol intake, Hemingway was enjoying better health than he had in a long while. His weight was down, his cholesterol was down, his blood pressure was down, and his spirits were up. Adding to that sunny outlook was his substantial progress on a memoir of his Paris years—published posthumously as *A Moveable Feast*—and the crisp, fresh air and good hunting of Idaho. All in all, he told a correspondent, he was feeling "like the best of the old days."[40] Indeed, he was feeling so expansive that he did something that fall

20

**The Hemingway image
perhaps best known to Americans**
Yousuf Karsh (born 1908), gelatin silver print, 34.2 x 27.3 cm (13 ½ x 10 ¾ in.), 1957. Ernest Hemingway Collection, John F. Kennedy Library, Boston, Massachusetts

that he generally avoided: despite a strong aversion to talking about his work, he consented to a question-answer session with a local Catholic youth group that was eager to know how the great man did it.

Bryson and his camera were thus intruding on the Hemingway household with its master at his congenial best, and the photographer found himself welcomed as a long-lost friend. Although Bryson turned down an invitation to stay with the Hemingways, he did take his meals with them, and he was soon joining Hemingway for afternoon strolls down to the nearby Sun Valley Lodge, where Hemingway "held court" in the bar.[41] Amid all the hospitable cheer, Bryson was not eager to leave, and his quick visit to Ketchum became a stay of five or six days.

Not surprisingly, the photographer began turning his camera on the author, and not long after he returned home, he sent the Hemingways a generous selection of the pictures he had shot of both of them. Commenting on the ones of her husband in a thank-you letter to Bryson, Mary numbered them among the "very best" ever done of him. Hemingway, on the other hand, was more reserved in his praise, and in a postscript penned at the bottom of his wife's letter, he wrote, "Mary thinks they're better than I do." Still, he admitted that they were "damned good."[42]

Like many a photojournalist, Bryson had a special affection for pictures capturing the unexpected or spontaneous moment, and the Hemingway shot that the subject liked best was a perfect example. It was afternoon, and Bryson and Hemingway were walking down the road, headed to the Sun Valley Lodge for a few drinks. Hemingway spotted a beer can and went to pick it up. Bryson, sensing that something out of the ordinary was going to happen, poised his camera, and as Hemingway kicked the can with all the vigor of "a high school football player," he caught the moment forever on film.[43]

It was easy to see why Hemingway liked the picture and why he later asked Bryson for several copies to send to friends. On the one hand, this image of a middle-aged man behaving like a teenager struck a note of humorous whimsy. By the same token, it was whimsy with a message informing the world that although he had not published much of anything lately, there was life in the old writer yet.

Another likeness among the Bryson photographs was much less reassuring about the state of Hemingway's durability. It was a close-up shot of his face, similar in composition to the Karsh portrait made about two years earlier (figure 21). But the impact was quite different. Whereas Karsh's image resonated with authoritative vigor, Bryson's was tentative, almost waiflike.

Roughly two and a half years after this picture was taken, Hemingway committed suicide following a precipitous decline in his mental stability. It is perhaps dangerous to look at this portrait armed with that knowledge. Nevertheless, its touching sense of frailty is as inescapable as it is haunting, and it is impossible to avoid the feeling that Bryson had unwittingly recorded a portent of the unhappiness and tragedy of Hemingway's last few years of life.

21
John Bryson's close-up portrait of Hemingway
John Bryson (born 1923), gelatin silver print, 30.4 x 24.1 cm (14 x 9 ½ in.), 1958/1959. Ernest Hemingway Collection, John F. Kennedy Library, Boston, Massachusetts. Copyright © John Bryson

NOTES

1. Raeburn, *Fame Became of Him*, p. 147.

2. Henry Strater, "Hemingway," *Art in America*, April 1961, pp. 84–85. For information on Strater and his relationship with Hemingway, see Michael Culver, "Sparring in the Dark: Hemingway, Strater and *The Old Man and the Sea*," *Hemingway Review* (spring 1992): 31–37; Michael Culver, "The Art of Henry Strater: An Examination of the Illustrations for Pound's *A Draft of XVI. Cantos*," *Paideuma* 12 (fall–winter 1983): 447–78; Gary Schwan, "Looking Back at 'Old Henry,'" *Palm Beach Life* (May 1988), pp. 68–71; Brian, *True Gen*.

3. Hemingway, *Moveable Feast*, p. 12.

4. Ibid., p. 35.

5. Man Ray, *Self Portrait* (Boston: Little, Brown, 1963), p. 184.

6. Reynolds, *Paris Years*, p. 245.

7. Baker, *Letters*, p. 223.

8. Max Perkins to Ernest Hemingway, November 10, 1927, Hemingway-Perkins correspondence, Scribner's Collection, Princeton University Library.

9. The best source for what little is known about Helen Breaker is the biography of her friend Hadley Richardson Hemingway: Diliberto, *Hadley*.

10. Dorothy Parker, "The Artist's Reward," *New Yorker* (November 30, 1929), p. 28.

11. The best source on Waldo Peirce is *Waldo Peirce, 1884–1970: A Centenary Exhibition*, with essay by Marius B. Péladeau (Rockland, Maine: William A. Farnsworth Library and Art Museum, 1984).

12. Bruccoli, *Only Thing That Counts*, p. 72.

13. Maxwell Perkins to Ernest Hemingway, June 4, 1928, Perkins-Hemingway correspondence, Scribner's Collection, Princeton University Library.

14. *Book Chats*, September–October 1928, pp. 25–29; Henry S. Canby, "Story of the Brave," *Saturday Review of Literature*, October 12, 1929, p. 231.

15. Bruccoli, *Only Thing That Counts*, p. 78.

16. The most-cited example of Hemingway's use of the boxing-ring metaphor is Lillian Ross, "How Do You Like It Now, Gentlemen?" *New Yorker*, May 13, 1950, p. 35.

17. The photograph album of these pictures is in the Sylvia Beach Collection, Princeton University Library.

18. Max Eastman, "Bull in the Afternoon," *New Republic* (June 7, 1933), p. 96.

19. Reynolds, *1930s*, p. 139.

20. The best biographical source on Covarrubias is Adriana Williams, *Covarrubias* (Austin: University of Texas Press, 1994).

21. Frank Crowninshield to Miguel Covarrubias, December 28, 1933, Miguel Covarrubias archive, Universidad de las Americas, Puebla, Mexico.

22. Clifton Fadiman, "Ernest Hemingway: An American Byron," *Nation* (January 18, 1983), p. 63.

23. Ernest Hemingway, *Green Hills of Africa* (New York: Scribner, 1935), pp. 277, 291.

24. Donald Adams, review of *To Have and Have Not*, *New York Times Book Review* (October 17, 1937), p. 2; Malcolm Cowley, "Hemingway: Work in Progress," *New Republic* (October

20, 1937), pp. 305–6; Alfred Kazin, review of *To Have and Have Not*, *New York Herald Tribune Books* (October 17, 1937), p. 3.

25. *Newsweek* (March 6, 1937), p. 38.

26. *Newsweek* (April 3, 1937), p. 15; *Time* (April 5, 1937), pp. 21–22, 24, 26.

27. Robert Capa, *Slightly Out of Focus* (New York: Henry Holt, 1947), p. 137.

28. *Life* (March 25, 1940), p. 100.

29. Bruccoli, *Only Thing That Counts*, p. 253.

30. Baker, *Life Story*, p. 425.

31. John Groth, *Studio: Europe* (New York: Vanguard, 1945), pp. 202, 203, 220.

32. Baker, *Life Story*, p. 528.

33. Raeburn, *Fame Became of Him*, p. 148.

34. Earl Theisen to Ernest Hemingway, January 15, 1954, Ernest Hemingway Collection, John F. Kennedy Library.

35. Hemingway, *How It Was*, p. 412.

36. Ibid.

37. Earl Theisen to Ernest Hemingway, January 15, 1954, August 23, 1955, Hemingway Collection, John F. Kennedy Library.

38. Yousuf Karsh, *Karsh Portraits* (Boston: New York Graphic Society, 1990), p. 74.

39. Hemingway, *How It Was*, p. 508.

40. Baker, *Life Story*, p. 542.

41. Notes from author's conversation with John Bryson, December 12, 1997.

42. Mary Hemingway to John Bryson [early 1959], collection of John Bryson.

43. John Bryson, "Spontaneous Touch," *Popular Photography* (November 1960), p. 59.

A Life in Portraits

Young Hemingway, far right, with his family, 1906

Hemingway grew up in the affluent Chicago suburb of Oak Park, the son of a physician father and a musically inclined, strong-willed mother. He accepted the community's conservative universe, and nothing in his youth marked him for a writer whose cynicism and sexual frankness would be the source of dismay for many Oak Parkers. Among the most dismayed were his parents, who lamented their son's refusal to focus in his writing on the more morally uplifting aspects of life. When Hemingway's first novel, *The Sun Also Rises*, was due for discussion at her book club, his mother absented herself, unable to bear the shame of it all.

For his part, Hemingway came to detest his mother, whom he saw as domineering, and to disdain his father, whom he regarded as a weakling. Those judgments became the basis for one of his early short stories, "The Doctor and the Doctor's Wife." Although there is no mistaking that this devastatingly negative portrayal of a marriage was inspired by his parents, it was one of his few works that his father claimed to like.

Ernest Hemingway Collection, John F. Kennedy Library, Boston, Massachusetts

The house where Hemingway grew up

During his early childhood, Hemingway's family resided at the home of his maternal grandfather. In 1905 his parents began building the house seen here on Oak Park's Kenilworth Avenue. The eight-bedroom house did not rank among the suburb's grandest, but it was far from humble. Its most impressive feature was a large music room for Hemingway's mother, with a fifteen-foot ceiling and balcony.

Ernest Hemingway Collection, John F. Kennedy Library, Boston, Massachusetts

Young Hemingway fishing, summer 1905

The Hemingway family spent large portions of every summer at its cottage on Walloon Lake in Michigan. There young Ernest began learning early the joys of hunting and fishing. As a present for his third birthday, his father took him fishing for the first time. The expedition proved hugely successful. "He caught the biggest fish of the crowd," his mother reported. "He knows when he gets a bite and lands them all himself." By the time this picture was taken, a lifelong passion for the pleasures of field and stream was thus already well rooted.

The summers at Walloon gave Hemingway something else as well. Out of his memories of them eventually came the settings and characters for some of his finest short stories.

Unidentified photographer, gelatin silver sepia print from original negative, 18.7 x 24.1 cm (7 ⅜ x 9 ½ in.), 1941. Ernest Hemingway Collection, John F. Kennedy Library, Boston, Massachusetts [Baker, Life Story, p. 5]

**Hemingway on the beach of
a lake in Michigan, summer 1916**
Here young Hemingway looks every
bit the model for Nick Adams, the
young hero of Hemingway's many
short stories drawn from his youth-
ful experiences in Michigan.

*Ernest Hemingway Collection,
John F. Kennedy Library, Boston,
Massachusetts*

Hemingway at the time of his graduation from high school, 1917

According to the assessment in his senior high school yearbook, "None are to be found more clever than Ernie." The observation reflected the respect he had earned for his abilities both in academics and in such extracurricular endeavors as his editorship of the school newspaper. The next logical step following graduation seemed to be college, but Hemingway was having none of that. Eager to free himself of parental dependence and demands, he went instead to Kansas City, Missouri, and became a reporter for the *Kansas City Star*.

Ernest Hemingway Collection, John F. Kennedy Library, Boston, Massachusetts [Fenton, p. 14]

**Kansas City Star style
book for reporters**

When Hemingway began his
job at the *Kansas City Star* as a cub
reporter, one of the first things
handed to him was a printed sheet
of the rules governing the newspaper's prose style. After reading
and absorbing it, he recalled years
later, one was expected to abide by it
strictly. It was not a bad way to begin
a writing career, and many of the
precepts set down in this sheet stuck
with Hemingway for the rest of his
life. The ones that perhaps made the
strongest impression, in part because the *Star* observed them so as-
siduously, were to be found in the
sheet's first paragraph: "Use short
sentences. Use short first para-
graphs. Use vigorous English. Be
positive, not negative."

This booklet version of the style
sheet was published many years after Hemingway had left the *Star* and
was sent to him by Pete Wellington,
who was the newspaper's assistant
city editor when Hemingway worked
there.

*Ernest Hemingway Collection,
John F. Kennedy Library, Boston,
Massachusetts* [Fenton, p. 31]

Hemingway in his ambulance driver's uniform of World War I

In spring 1917 the United States became an active participant in World War I, and massive recruitment of American soldiers began. Hemingway wanted to enlist, but restrained by parental objections and an eye condition that would probably have precluded his acceptance, he never tried. Still, as the conflict progressed, he became determined that "a show like this" would not go on without him. By early May 1918 he had quit the *Star* and was in New York waiting to sail for Italy as a member of the Red Cross ambulance corps.

His stint with the ambulance corps proved short. On July 8, shortly after midnight, Hemingway was in the Italian front lines distributing coffee, candy, and postcards to soldiers. Suddenly, an Austrian trench mortar arced down, spewing its metal shards in all directions. Among the seriously wounded was Hemingway, who would sit out the rest of the war as a convalescent.

Gino-Fish studio of Chicago (active circa 1920), print made from original, 17 x 10.1 cm (6¾ x 4 in.), circa 1918. Ernest Hemingway Collection, John F. Kennedy Library, Boston, Massachusetts
[Baker, Life Story, p. 36]

Hemingway's first love, Agnes von Kurowsky

Among the Red Cross nurses attending to Hemingway as he recovered from his battle injuries was an American woman named Agnes von Kurowsky (1892?–1984). He flirted with all the nurses in the hospital, but the tall, slim Kurowsky was special. Before long he was in love with her. More than six years his senior, Kurowsky kept him at arm's length for awhile, but eventually she succumbed to his ebullient charm. In affectionate letters to him, she took to calling him Kid and referring to herself as Mrs. Kid. But Kurowsky's feelings for Hemingway were never as deep as his attachment to her, and she broke off the relationship in a letter not long after he returned home to Oak Park.

Hemingway's hurt over the breakup was still alive in the early 1920s when he wrote "A Very Short Story," a bitter tale clearly patterned on the romance with Kurowsky. Later she was a primary model for the heroine in his novel of World War I, *A Farewell to Arms*.

Unidentified photographer, gelatin silver print, 10.8 x 7.6 cm (4 ¼ x 3 in.), circa 1918. Ernest Hemingway Collection, John F. Kennedy Library, Boston, Massachusetts

Italian cross of merit awarded to Hemingway in World War I

Hemingway's experience in World War I gave rise to myths about him—fed by his own penchant for exaggeration—that died hard after he became famous. It was widely thought, for example, that he had been a lieutenant in the Italian army instead of an ambulance driver, with only a courtesy junior officer's rank, and that his wounding had left him with a metal kneecap.

Still, Hemingway's brush with death at the Italian front was heroic enough without those fabrications. His insistence, following his wounding, on disregarding his own pain to assist disabled soldiers around him was enough to earn him the Italian silver cross of merit.

Ernest Hemingway Collection, John F. Kennedy Library, Boston, Massachusetts

Hadley Richardson Hemingway

By mid-fall 1920, Hemingway was living in Chicago, sharing an apartment with a friend. Settled on becoming a writer, he was doing occasional pieces for the *Toronto Star*, where he had worked earlier in the year, and looking for steadier employment. In the midst of this uncertain existence, Hadley Richardson (1891–1979) came from St. Louis for a visit with mutual friends in Chicago.

Hemingway was much taken with this quietly attractive, auburn-haired woman, and she with him. By spring they were talking marriage and planning to go to Europe, where, cushioned by trust income from her family, he could pursue his writing ambitions. In September 1921 they were married, and in December they sailed for Paris.

Eight years his senior, Hadley proved unreservedly supportive of Hemingway's writing aspirations, and although their marriage lasted less than six years, he always regarded her with warmth and gratitude. Hadley returned the compliment, feeling that without his adventurous spirit her life would have been far more dull and narrow.

Helen Pierce Breaker (circa 1895–1938?), gelatin silver print, 22.2 x 17.8 cm (8 ¾ x 7 in.), 1928. Ernest Hemingway Collection, John F. Kennedy Library, Boston, Massachusetts

View from the kitchen window of the Hemingways' first apartment in Paris

When the Hemingways arrived in Paris, they were financially secure. Hadley's trust could be expected to yield an annual income of more than $3,000, and Hemingway's agreement to write stories for the *Toronto Star* promised to add substantially to that figure. They could afford decent housing at contemporary Paris prices. Yet when they went apartment hunting, they settled on a two-room, fourth-floor walk-up in the oldest part of the Paris Left Bank, which cost about eighteen dollars a month. The neighborhood was charmless, with no good restaurants or shopping, and the plumbing and heating were primitive. But the newlyweds indulged themselves in other ways. Immediately after moving into their apartment, they left for a three-week skiing holiday in Switzerland.

This view from the apartment may have been taken by Hemingway himself. In a letter to his parents, he called the apartment "the jolliest place you ever saw."

Unidentified photographer, gelatin silver print, 13.6 x 8 cm (5 ³/₈ x 3 ¹/₈ in.), circa 1922. Ernest Hemingway Collection, John F. Kennedy Library, Boston, Massachusetts [Reynolds, *Paris Years*, p. 17]

**Hemingway outside his
second apartment in Paris,
1924**

When this picture was taken, little
of Hemingway's fiction had found
its way onto the printed page. His
potential was nevertheless well respected in the Anglo-American literary community of Paris. The poet
Ezra Pound was recommending him
as "the finest prose stylist in the
world," and the novelist and literary
review editor Ford Madox Ford later
recalled, "I did not read more than
six words of his before I decided to
publish everything he sent me."

*Ernest Hemingway Collection,
John F. Kennedy Library, Boston,
Massachusetts* [Baker, Life
Story, pp. 123, 126]

Sherwood Anderson

A leading figure of the so-called Chicago Renaissance, Sherwood Anderson (1874–1941) was reaching the height of his prominence as a chronicler of the darker side of American life when Hemingway met him through a mutual friend in Chicago in 1920. Anderson thought well of the young man's potential, and he counseled Hemingway that the best milieu in Europe for perfecting his craft was the Anglo-American literary community in Paris. When Hemingway finally decided to heed that advice, Anderson provided his young friend with letters of introduction to three members of that Paris community—the bookshop proprietor Sylvia Beach, the poet Ezra Pound, and Gertrude Stein, the writer of esoteric prose whose home was a gathering place for the city's avant-garde. Four years later, Anderson helped to persuade his own publishers to bring out the first major volume of Hemingway's short stories, *In Our Time*.

But gratitude was not among Hemingway's most conspicuous virtues, and his friendship with Anderson had chilled in 1926, when he published *Torrents of Spring*, an obvious parody of Anderson's work.

Alfred Stieglitz (1864–1946), gelatin silver print, 22.9 x 18.4 cm (9 x 7¼ in.), 1923. National Portrait Gallery, Smithsonian Institution, Washington, D.C.

Gertrude Stein

One of the most momentous relationships that Hemingway formed during his first months in Paris was his friendship with the avant-garde art collector and experimental Modernist writer Gertrude Stein (1874–1946). In contrast to the many who found Stein's prose incomprehensible, Hemingway respected her professional expertise, and he readily adopted her as a mentor. From her he learned much about the rhythm of words and the power of repetition and unembellished direct statement. But the flow of benefits was two-way, and eventually Hemingway was instrumental in getting some of Stein's work published.

The friendship, however, had soured by late 1926, and the final chapter in the Hemingway-Stein relationship is an exchange of potshots. In her 1933 *Autobiography of Alice B. Toklas*, Stein called Hemingway "yellow." Not long afterward, Hemingway counterattacked in *Green Hills of Africa*, belittling Stein's need to malign the man who had *taught her* to write.

Jo Davidson (1883–1952), terra-cotta, 27.9 cm (11 in.), 1922/1923. National Portrait Gallery, Smithsonian Institution, Washington, D.C. [Stein, p. 265]

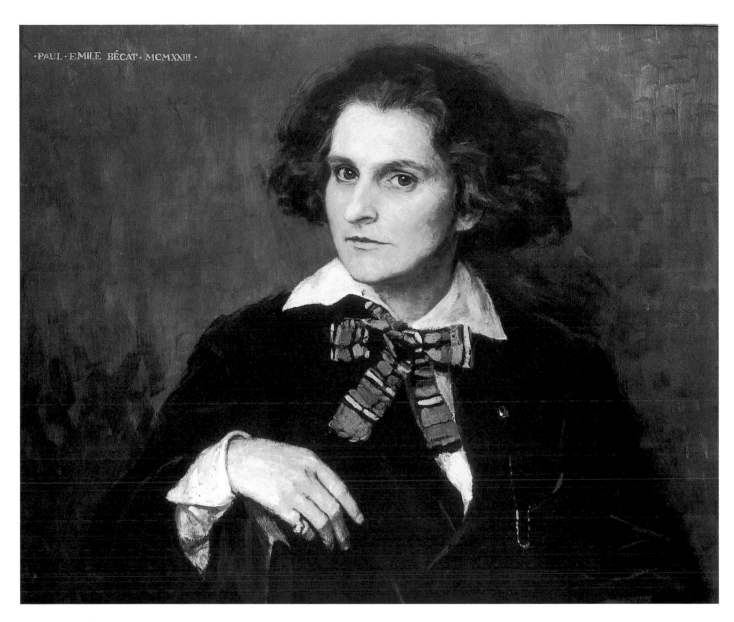

Sylvia Beach

One of Hemingway's favorite haunts in Paris was Shakespeare and Company, a bookshop and lending library in the rue de l'Odéon specializing in English and American literature, and a center of the city's Anglo-American literary community. The shop's proprietor was Sylvia Beach (1887–1962), who, when Hemingway met her in late 1921, was overseeing one of the major events in twentieth-century Western literature. Because the sexual frankness of the Irish writer James Joyce's *Ulysses* precluded its publication in the British Isles, Beach took on its publication herself, and in early 1922 this salient and controversial work of fiction finally came out.

Beach and Hemingway took to each other immediately, and she was among the first to appreciate "his originality [and . . .] storyteller's gift." His affection for her expressed itself in attempts to introduce her to the joys of spectator sports. Beach did not care much for the sports, but she liked Hemingway so much that she gladly tolerated his efforts to broaden her horizons.

This portrait of Beach was the work of Paul-Émile Bécat, brother-in-law of Beach's longtime companion Adrienne Monnier.

Paul-Émile Bécat (1885–1960), oil on canvas, 57.1 x 63.5 cm (22 ½ x 25 in.), 1923. Sylvia Beach Collection, Department of Rare Books and Special Collections, Princeton University Library, Princeton, New Jersey [Fitch, p. 148]

James Joyce

One of the first local literary figures of whom Hemingway became aware after settling in Paris was the Irish short story and novel writer James Joyce (1882–1941), who had been living there since 1920. In his first year and a half in the city, in fact, Hemingway read all of Joyce's major works and even helped to solicit subscriptions for *Ulysses*. The two men became occasional drinking pals, and on a few of their sprees, Hemingway ended up having to carry Joyce home. Joyce also influenced Hemingway's direction as a writer. It was in the work of the Irish writer, for example, that Hemingway began to find ways to start a short story with greater directness, and in his novel *To Have and Have Not*, there are passages that clearly owe a debt to *Ulysses*. Hemingway once said of Joyce, "He could write better than anyone I knew."

Berenice Abbott (1898–1991), photograph, 34.3 x 26.7 cm (13½ x 10½ in.), 1928. Berenice Abbott / Commerce Graphics Ltd., Inc., East Rutherford, New Jersey [Meyers, p. 83]

Ezra Pound

Ezra Pound (1885–1972) was a poet by profession, but he was a generous counselor by instinct, and many a writer, among them T. S. Eliot and James Joyce, benefited greatly from his advice, encouragement, and editing. Pound met Hemingway early in 1922 and quickly took him on as a protégé. From Pound, Hemingway learned "to distrust adjectives" and received valuable guidance in how to compress his words into precise images. In contrast to the many friends and mentors whom Hemingway later turned on, Pound's name always evoked pleasant memories. In *A Moveable Feast*, the memoir of his Paris years, he called Pound "a sort of saint" and claimed he was "the man I liked and trusted the most as critic."

This drawing is one of many likenesses of Pound done by his good friend Wyndham Lewis, originator of the British brand of cubism, which Pound had christened vorticism. By the time Lewis did this drawing, he had moved away from vorticism toward a more representational style.

Percy Wyndham Lewis (1884–1957), pencil on paper, 25.3 x 17.8 cm (10 x 7 in.), circa 1920. Art Collection, Harry Ransom Humanities Research Center, The University of Texas at Austin [Moveable Feast, pp. 108, 134]

Hemingway's
Three Stories & Ten Poems,
1923

The edition of Hemingway's
first book, *Three Stories & Ten Poems*,
amounted to only three hundred
copies, and the chief marketing
outlet was Sylvia Beach's shop.
Nevertheless, it did get some no-
tices. In a review for the Paris edition of the *Chicago Tribune*, Gertrude
Stein judged that he should "stick to
poetry." On the other hand, the literary magazine *the transatlantic review*
thought that his stories demonstra-
ted "a sensitive feeling for the emotional possibilities of a situation."

Ernest Hemingway Collection,
John F. Kennedy Library, Boston,
Massachusetts   [Reynolds, Paris Years,
p. 153; Hanneman, p. 345]

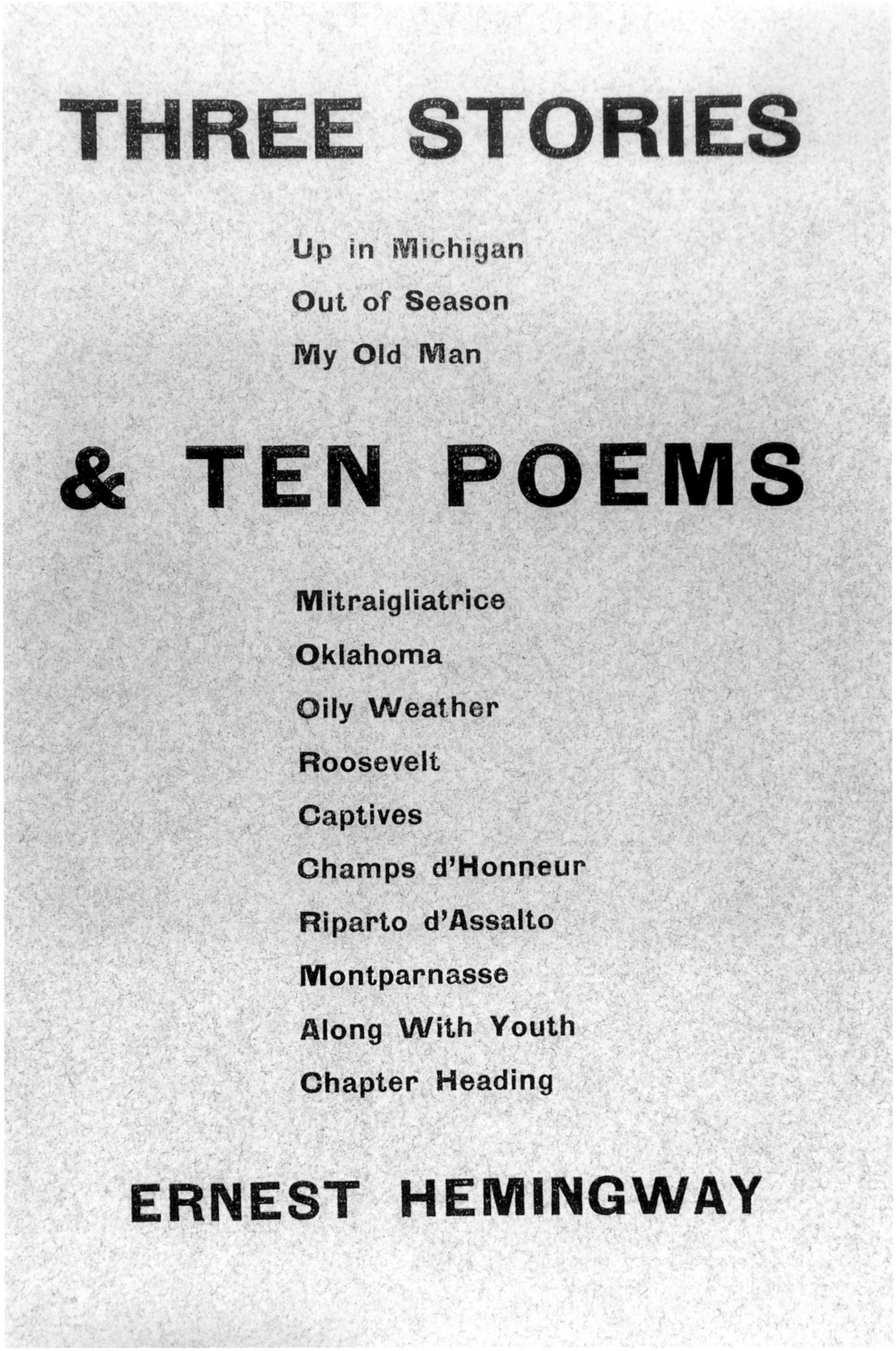

THREE STORIES

Up in Michigan
Out of Season
My Old Man

& TEN POEMS

Mitraigliatrice
Oklahoma
Oily Weather
Roosevelt
Captives
Champs d'Honneur
Riparto d'Assalto
Montparnasse
Along With Youth
Chapter Heading

ERNEST HEMINGWAY

the author   *wood-cut from portrait by henry strater*

in our time

by

ernest hemingway

A GIRL IN CHICAGO: Tell us about the French women, Hank. What are they like?

BILL SMITH: How old are the French women, Hank?

paris:

printed at the three mountains press *and for sale at* shakespeare & company, *in the rue de l'odéon*; *london:* william jackson, *took's court, cursitor street, chancery lane.*

1924

Frontispiece and title page of Hemingway's *in our time*, 1924

Also published by a small, independent press in Paris, the second volume of Hemingway's work, *in our time*, consisted of small, carefully honed descriptive vignettes that focused largely on violence and war. The book numbered thirty-two pages and came out in an edition of 170. One of the few who saw it was critic Edmund Wilson, to whom Hemingway had sent a copy. In a review, Wilson declared that, little or not, the book had "more artistic dignity than any other . . . by an American about the period of the war."

Ernest Hemingway Collection, John F. Kennedy Library, Boston, Massachusetts   [*Reynolds, Paris Years, p. 243*]

F. Scott Fitzgerald

When Hemingway first met F. Scott Fitzgerald (1896–1940) in Paris in spring 1925, Fitzgerald had just published his finest work, *The Great Gatsby*, and was at the height of his reputation as one of America's leading young writers. Even before they began to talk, he was prepared to like Hemingway, for he had seen *in our time* and admired it greatly. On the strength of that slim volume, he had recommended its author as "the real thing" to his editor, Max Perkins, at Charles Scribner's Sons. As the friendship developed, Fitzgerald continued to take an interest in furthering Hemingway's career, and thanks partly to his urgings, the prestigious Scribner finally took Hemingway on as one of its writers in 1926.

That good turn, however, was not enough to keep the friendship on solid footings as Hemingway's star rose and Fitzgerald's fell. Ultimately, Hemingway became scornful of Fitzgerald, and in the first printed version of his story "The Snows of Kilimanjaro" was a passage characterizing Fitzgerald as a writer ruined by his naive fascination with the rich. Soon after the story's appearance in *Esquire* in 1936, Fitzgerald fired off a letter to Hemingway telling him to "lay off."

David Silvette (1909–92), oil on canvas, 61 x 50.8 cm (24 x 20 in.), 1935. National Portrait Gallery, Smithsonian Institution, Washington, D.C.   [Baker, Life Story, p. 144; Reynolds, 1930s, p. 223]

Max Perkins

By the time Max Perkins (1884–1947) died, his reputation as the nurturing editor of distinguished writers was legend in American publishing. Of the author-editor relationships making up that legend, few loomed more prominently than the one he formed with Hemingway in early 1926. When Perkins recruited him into the Charles Scribner's Sons stable of writers, Hemingway was hardly a proven quantity, and it was mostly intuition that led Perkins to advance money for a novel that he had not seen. That intuition proved remarkably sound. The novel was *The Sun Also Rises*, and its publication marked Hemingway's arrival as one of America's most promising young writers.

Perkins was never an aggressive amender of Hemingway's work. Generally, he did little more than offer advice, which was only sometimes taken. He did put his foot down, however, to limit Hemingway's use of profanities to only those most essential to his writing. Hemingway claimed, in the name of realism, that they had to be there. Perkins understood that argument. Yet he also knew that the reading public would not accept as much raciness on the printed page as Hemingway would have liked.

Unidentified photographer, gelatin silver print, circa 1930. Charles Scribner's Collection, Department of Rare Books and Special Collections, Princeton University Library, Princeton, New Jersey

Hemingway with his second wife, Pauline Pfeiffer

The daughter of a rich Arkansas landowner and banker, Pauline Pfeiffer (1894–1951) found Hemingway too coarse for her taste when she first met him in early 1925, and Hemingway was much more taken with Pauline's sister than with her. Pauline's friendship with Hemingway's wife Hadley, however, threw them together and ultimately became a subterfuge for pursuing their own relationship. By early 1926 their initial indifference had turned into strong mutual attraction, and at year's end, with his divorce from Hadley in the works, the two were planning to marry.

Pauline was unflagging in her efforts to cater to Hemingway's wants. But eventually her ministrations were not enough to curb her husband's wandering eye. By the late 1930s, as yet another woman entered Hemingway's life, his second marriage was disintegrating.

Unidentified photographer, gelatin silver print, 7.5 x 10.8 cm (3 x 4¼ in.), circa 1927.
Ernest Hemingway Collection, John F. Kennedy Library, Boston, Massachusetts

John Dos Passos

One of the most experimental among American Modernist writers of the 1920s and 1930s, John Dos Passos (1896–1970) may have first run into Hemingway during World War I when both were ambulance drivers. At least that is what the two men liked to think. But their first definite meeting occurred in Paris in 1923. Dos Passos did not share Hemingway's passion for sports, but in other respects they were quite compatible. Their friendship became all the closer when Dos Passos married one of Hemingway's chums from his Michigan summers, Katy Smith.

As with most of Hemingway's literary relationships, the one with Dos Passos eventually deteriorated. The turning point was a disagreement in 1937 over the leftist elements in the Spanish civil war. After that, Hemingway took to referring to Dos Passos as "the one-eyed Portuguese bastard." At one point, the friendship seemed on the mend, but after Dos Passos portrayed a Hemingwaylike character in *Chosen Country* as an unlikable bully, chances for reconciliation passed. In *A Moveable Feast*, Hemingway returned the compliment by characterizing Dos Passos as a "pilot fish," who connived with others to destroy his marriage to Hadley.

Unidentified photographer, gelatin silver print, 15.4 x 10.2 cm (6 1/16 x 4 in.), circa 1935. National Portrait Gallery, Smithsonian Institution, Washington, D.C.   [Movcablc Fcast, pp. 206–8]

Charles Scribner

After signing on with Charles Scribner's Sons in 1926, Hemingway remained with the publishing house for the rest of his life. One of his most cherished Scribner connections was his relationship with Charles Scribner (1890–1952), who became president of the firm in 1932. Among the evidences of the friendship were the many rambling and spontaneous letters that Hemingway wrote to Scribner, discoursing on everything from his sex life and his hatred for his mother to the progress of his work.

Generally, the tone of these missives was amiable. On a few occasions, however, it became decidedly testy, as in 1948, when Hemingway responded to a 10 percent royalty offer on a new edition of some of his novels. Feeling angry and underappreciated, he declared: "I am an old horse like Exterminator that won for you every time but once. And I won't run for ten percent and you have that straight from [the] horse's mouth. . . . The only thing that makes horses like Exterminator and me sore is when . . . the people that start you haven't got the guts to bet." But even in the midst of these rantings, he made sure to remind Scribner of how "very fond" he was of him.

Charles Scribner Jr. (1921–1995), gelatin silver print, 26.6 x 35.5 cm (10 ½ x 14 in.), circa 1936. Collection of Charles Scribner III
[Baker, Letters, pp. 637–38]

Program from annual festival and bullfights in Pamplona, 1924

In 1923 Hemingway went to Spain with a couple of friends and saw his first bullfight. He was so taken with both the country and this ancient blood sport that within a month he returned with his wife to witness the daily round of bullfights that highlighted the annual fiesta of San Fermin in Pamplona. By the time the festival was over, bullfighting was one of the passions of his life, and his returns to Pamplona at fiesta time over the next few years only deepened that passion.

Ernest Hemingway Collection, John F. Kennedy Library, Boston, Massachusetts

PAMPLONA 1924

FERIAS Y FIESTAS DE SAN FERMIN

Programa de festejos que se celebrarán del 6 al 18 de Julio

Hemingway trying his hand at bullfighting in Pamplona, 1924

The professional bullfights in Pamplona began in late afternoon. But each morning, fans wishing to live out their matador fantasies could join amateur free-for-alls with bulls whose horns had been padded. Hemingway's conviction that bullfighting was an ultimate test of courage, and his own perennial eagerness to prove his bravery, made it inevitable that he should enter the fray. At Pamplona in 1924 he participated in the free-for-alls five times by his count, and in the picture here he can be seen (right of center, in white pants and dark sweater) facing a charging bull. Hemingway viewed these events more seriously than most and took great pride in his attempts to replicate the moves of a trained matador.

Unidentified photographer, gelatin silver print, 12.7 x 17.7 cm (5 x 7 in.), 1924.
Ernest Hemingway Collection, John F. Kennedy Library, Boston, Massachusetts

Early edition of
The Sun Also Rises

The late spring of 1925 was an unproductive period for Hemingway. He had recently finished the last story for his first full-scale volume of short stories, *In Our Time*, and did not much feel like tackling something new. But the bullfights and carousing of his third visit to Pamplona's festival in July gave him a creative lift. Within a month of the festival's end, he was working out the draft of his first novel. Set in Pamplona and peopled with characters patterned on individuals who had just been there with Hemingway, the work depicted the cynicism and drift of the "lost generation" that had spawned in the tragic waste of World War I. The world soon knew it as *The Sun Also Rises*.

The dissoluteness of the characters in *The Sun Also Rises* led one reviewer to charge Hemingway with hiding his talents "under a bushel of sensationalism and triviality." Another school of opinion found its publication one of the most exciting literary events of the year, and one critic claimed that its "lean, hard narrative prose" put a good deal of "literary English to shame."

Department of Rare Books and Special Collections, Princeton University Library, Princeton, New Jersey [Hanneman, pp. 350, 352]

First edition of
A Farewell to Arms, 1929

Drawn heavily from Hemingway's own experiences as an ambulance driver in World War I, A Farewell to Arms cast its author in a new light. Until its publication in 1929, Hemingway had been seen as a talented writer with great promise. Now, heralded by reviews filled with superlatives, he was a widely acknowledged master of modern prose. After reading A Farewell to Arms, his friend the poet Archibald MacLeish wrote: "I am afraid you are not only a fine writer which I have always known but something a lot more than that & it scares me."

Department of Rare Books and Special Collections, Princeton University Library, Princeton, New Jersey [Reynolds, 1930s, p. 11]

Circular announcing the serialization of *A Farewell to Arms*

Hemingway's publisher, Charles Scribner's Sons, tried to limit the profanities and allusions to sex in his works, but it did not seek to excise such elements entirely, for fear of jeopardizing the integrity of his writing. That attempt to strike a balance between the vestiges of Victorian conventionality and modernity's taste for greater frankness was not good enough for some. When the June 1929 issue of *Scribner's magazine*, containing the second installment of *A Farewell to Arms*, reached Boston newsstands, the police promptly seized it because Hemingway's story of love and war was deemed salacious. The next issue of the magazine, with installment three, fared no better.

Charges of lewdness were not new to Hemingway. Shortly after the publication of *The Sun Also Rises* in 1926, he had received a letter declaring it "a doubtful honor" to be the author of "one of the filthiest books of the year." It was signed by his mother.

Charles Scribner's Collection, Department of Rare Books and Special Collections, Princeton University Library, Princeton, New Jersey [Baker, *Life Story*, p. 180]

From a photograph by Helen Breaker

The eagerly awaited New Novel by

ERNEST HEMINGWAY

"A FAREWELL TO ARMS"

begins in the

May SCRIBNER'S Magazine

A vivid love story woven into the texture of the debacle of Italian retreat. The sharp, direct, Hemingway style which distinguishes "The Sun Also Rises" and his stories in "Men Without Women," with an added power.

THREE GREAT STORIES NOW RUNNING IN SCRIBNER'S
An African Savage's Own Story — Mad Anthony Wayne — A Farewell to Arms

100,000 HOMES WILL "DOG-EAR" THIS MAY NUMBER OF THE NEW SCRIBNER'S MAGAZINE

Martha Gellhorn

In late 1936 Ernest Hemingway met the writer Martha Gellhorn (1908–98) in a bar in Key West, Florida. In her late twenties, she was blonde, pretty, and successful, and Hemingway was attracted from the start. By early the next year, she had joined him in Spain, where he was covering the civil war for the North American News Alliance. Their relationship blossomed into a full-blown affair. Ultimately, Hemingway's marriage to his second wife, Pauline, collapsed under the weight of this new relationship. In late 1940, soon after his divorce became final, he married Gellhorn.

Gellhorn had professional ambitions of her own, however, and she was disinclined to cater to her husband's wants. This was quite a contrast to Hemingway's previous two wives, whose chief concern had been keeping him happy. In the end, it was a contrast he could not abide. By the time Gellhorn divorced him in 1945, the marriage was long over.

Unidentified photographer, gelatin silver print, 15.5 x 20.3 cm (6 ⅛ x 8 in.), circa 1940.
Ernest Hemingway Collection, John F. Kennedy Library, Boston, Massachusetts

Martha Gellhorn with Robert Merriman, member of an international volunteer brigade fighting for Spain's Loyalist cause

On his trips to Spain during the civil war, Hemingway's main business was to report on the conflict for a news syndicate. But he was also storing up memories of events, terrain, and people for use in future works of fiction. One figure he studied closely was Major Robert Merriman, pictured here with Martha Gellhorn. A California history professor, Merriman was one of the many Americans who flocked to Spain to aid the Loyalist cause, and when Hemingway met him in 1937, he was chief of staff in one of the international brigades. Merriman eventually died in the war, but he enjoys a kind of immortality as the model for Robert Jordan, the hero of Hemingway's major portrayal of the civil war, *For Whom the Bell Tolls*.

Ernest Hemingway Collection, John F. Kennedy Library, Boston, Massachusetts

First edition of
***For Whom the Bell Tolls,* 1940**

Much of Hemingway's work after *A Farewell to Arms* in 1929 met with heavy criticism, and by the late 1930s many thought that his creative powers were spent. That school of opinion lost its credibility in the fall of 1940 with the publication of his novel of the Spanish civil war, *For Whom the Bell Tolls.* From the outset, the book was a best-seller, and more than one critic discussed its merits almost as if it was already a classic. One reviewer called it "the fullest, deepest, truest" book that Hemingway had ever written and predicted that it would eventually rank among "the major novels in American literature."

Department of Rare Books and Special Collections, Princeton University Library, Princeton, New Jersey [Hanneman, p. 403]

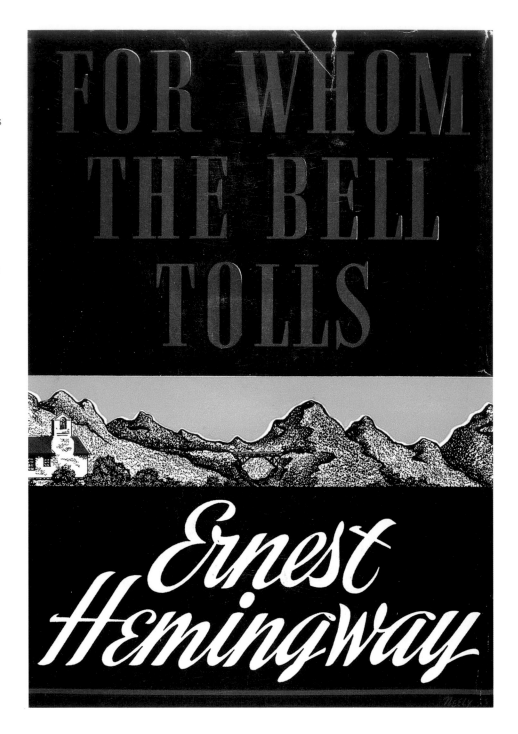

Hemingway showing off his marlin catch with his friend, the American bullfighter Sidney Franklin (in beret)

Hemingway's passion for hunting and fishing ran as deeply as his passion for writing, and although his literary endeavors were the main source of his fame, his celebrity rested as well on his reputation as an avid and able outdoor sportsman. By the mid-1930s, when this picture was taken on a pier in Key West, Florida, he was on his way to becoming the best-known fisherman in America. He was also becoming a pacesetter in developing new and more aggressive techniques in deep-sea fishing, which, according to one expert, ultimately transformed the sport.

Ernest Hemingway Collection, John F. Kennedy Library, Boston, Massachusetts

Hemingway hunting in Idaho

Hemingway's love of hunting inevitably drew him to the vast, unpopulated expanses of the West, where game was plentiful. In 1939 he discovered Idaho, and he is shown here in 1941 hunting for pheasant in the area around Sun Valley, the state's newly developed resort for outdoor enthusiasts.

The picture was taken by Robert Capa, who had photographed Hemingway during the Spanish civil war. It was part of a series of photographs taken for a *Life* spread entitled "Life Goes Hunting at Sun Valley." The other person featured in the spread was the actor Gary Cooper, who was soon to play the lead in the screen version of *For Whom the Bell Tolls*.

Robert Capa (1913–54), gelatin silver print (detail), 34.2 x 23.1 cm (13⅞ x 9⅛ in.), 1941. National Portrait Gallery, Smithsonian Institution, Washington, D.C. Copyright © Robert Capa Archives, ICP

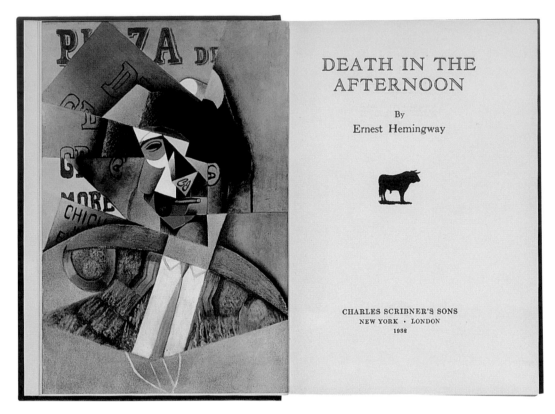

First edition of *Death in the Afternoon*

Hemingway's discourse on bullfighting, *Death in the Afternoon*, met with mixed reviews. One critic found its prose style "irritating" and its "'he-mannish'" tone "brutal and infuriating." Another described the book as "teeming with life, vigorous, powerful, moving, and consistently entertaining." But one point was indisputable: Hemingway knew his subject and had produced one of the most authoritative accounts of bullfighting ever written in English.

For the frontispiece of *Death in the Afternoon*, Hemingway chose a painting that he had added to his own modest collection of modern European art in 1932, just as the book was being prepared for publication. It was the work of the Spanish-born cubist painter Juan Gris, whom Hemingway had known in Paris in the 1920s. Painted in 1913 and titled *The Bullfighter*, the picture incorporated lettering from bullfight posters, and the CHICU in the middle left probably refers to the matador Manuel Gimenez, nicknamed Chicuelo.

Collection of Albert J. DeFazio III   [*Hanneman, pp. 370, 373*]

Hemingway, foreground, at the Hotel Scribe in Paris during World War II

As a correspondent during World War II, Hemingway covered the Normandy invasion, the advance on Paris, and the first stages of Allied penetration into Germany. In between, he did a good deal of carousing, and in the picture here, by *Life* war artist Floyd Davis, he is seen at the center table, holding forth in the bar at the Hotel Scribe in Paris, a major watering hole for war correspondents in the fall of 1944. Seated with him are *New Yorker* writer Janet Flanner and CBS newsman William Shirer.

Floyd Davis (1896–1966), oil on canvas, 48.3 x73.7 cm (19 x 29 in.), 1944. National Portrait Gallery, Smithsonian Institution, Washington, D.C.

Mary Welsh Hemingway

Hemingway's marriage to Martha Gellhorn had difficulties from its outset in 1940, and its dissolution became certain when he met Mary Welsh (1908–86) shortly after he arrived in England to begin covering World War II. The attractive, petite Welsh worked for *Time*, and Hemingway began courting her practically from the moment a friend introduced her at a London restaurant. Among Welsh's most alluring qualities was a willingness to flatter and cater to him—a quality that meshed perfectly with Hemingway's unrelenting need to occupy a superior position in his relationships.

The courtship had its tempestuous moments and almost ended at the Ritz Hotel in Paris when, in a fit of jealous rage over Welsh's estranged husband, a well-lubricated Hemingway shot up a toilet bowl. By the time Hemingway left Europe early in 1945, however, he and Welsh were planning to be married.

Unidentified photographer, gelatin silver print, 15.8 x 11.4 cm (6 ¼ x 4 ½ in.), circa 1944. Ernest Hemingway Collection, John F. Kennedy Library, Boston, Massachusetts

Hemingway studying a map in France shortly before the Allied entry into Paris

By all accounts, Hemingway thoroughly enjoyed his opportunity to play soldier during World War II by engaging in reconnaissance with French resistance fighters. International conventions expressly forbade such activity on the part of war correspondents, and eventually the U.S. Army ordered an investigation into his all too soldierlike doings. But authorities did not relish coming down too hard on America's most celebrated writer. In the end they accepted—without too much effort to refute it—his claim that his association with the resistance was strictly limited to news-gathering functions.

Unidentified photographer, gelatin silver print, 19.7 x 22.8 cm (7¾ x 9 in.), 1944.
Ernest Hemingway Collection, John F. Kennedy Library, Boston, Massachusetts

Hemingway having breakfast at his home in Cuba

Called Finca Vigía (Lookout Farm) and discovered by his third wife, Martha Gellhorn, Hemingway's home in Cuba was modestly palatial, boasting extensive gardens, a tennis court, and a swimming pool. It also had a large cat population, which roamed the estate freely. In the picture here, Hemingway takes an early-morning breakfast in his bedroom in the company of several of his favorite cats. Above him hangs *The Guitar Player* by Juan Gris, one of a number of distinguished modern paintings that the writer had collected in the 1920s and 1930s.

This image was first published with Malcolm Cowley's "Portrait of Mr. Papa," which ran in *Life* magazine early in 1949. A combination of fact, exaggeration, and outright misinformation, the piece added substantially to Hemingway's repute with its depiction of a kind of multitalented superman—as capable a military strategist, for example, as he was a writer.

George Leavens (active 1940s), photograph (detail), 1949. George Leavens | Life magazine. Copyright © Time Inc.

Hemingway with Adriana Ivancich

Pictured here with Hemingway at his home in Cuba is Adriana Ivancich, member of an aristocratic Venetian family. From the moment he met this young girl during his Italian stay in 1948, Hemingway was smitten, and over the next several years, he carried on a platonic flirtation with her that may well have become more serious had she permitted. The advent of Adriana marked the end of a dry spell in Hemingway's writing, and their relationship became the basis for the May–December romance portrayed in *Across the River and into the Trees*. Adriana also seems to have had a part in the making of one of Hemingway's master-pieces, *The Old Man and the Sea*. For it was her stay with the Hemingways in late 1950 that provided the energizing lift that the writer apparently needed to begin this tale.

Ernest Hemingway Collection, John F. Kennedy Library, Boston, Massachusetts

First edition of

Across the River and into the Trees

Following his stint as a correspondent during World War II, Hemingway had a hard time getting his creative bearings, and his novel-writing efforts over the next several years yielded nothing publishable. Finally, inspired largely by a stay in Venice in 1948, he began a tale set in that city, about a fiftyish American army colonel and his affair with a young Italian girl. Titling the work *Across the River and into the Trees*, Hemingway thought it was the best book he had ever written. Unfortunately, most critics saw it differently, and reviews of the novel featured such adjectives as "lamentable" and "disappointing." Admiration for Hemingway's past accomplishments was such that a few critics could not resist introducing a ray of hope into their dismal appraisals. "It is wonderful to know," observed one, "that this book is not his last word."

Department of Rare Books and Special Collections, Princeton University Library, Princeton, New Jersey [Hanneman, pp. 425–27]

Source for *The Old Man and the Sea,* Carlos Gutiérrez, aboard Hemingway's boat, the *Pilar*

A commercial fisherman working out of Havana, Carlos Gutiérrez met Hemingway in 1932, and for a number of years he hired out as chief mate on Hemingway's fishing expeditions around Cuba. Hemingway's skill as a deep-sea fisherman benefited from Gutiérrez, and so did his literary fortunes. In the mid-1930s Gutiérrez told him the story of an aging fisherman who, after wrestling for days to bring in a huge fish, ultimately lost his prize to sharks. Hemingway thought the tale had wonderful fictional possibilities, but he hesitated to use it for fear of failing to do it justice. Finally, in January 1950, it began taking shape as *The Old Man and the Sea*, and at the center of the story was a character patterned partly on Gutiérrez.

Ernest Hemingway Collection, John F. Kennedy Library, Boston, Massachusetts

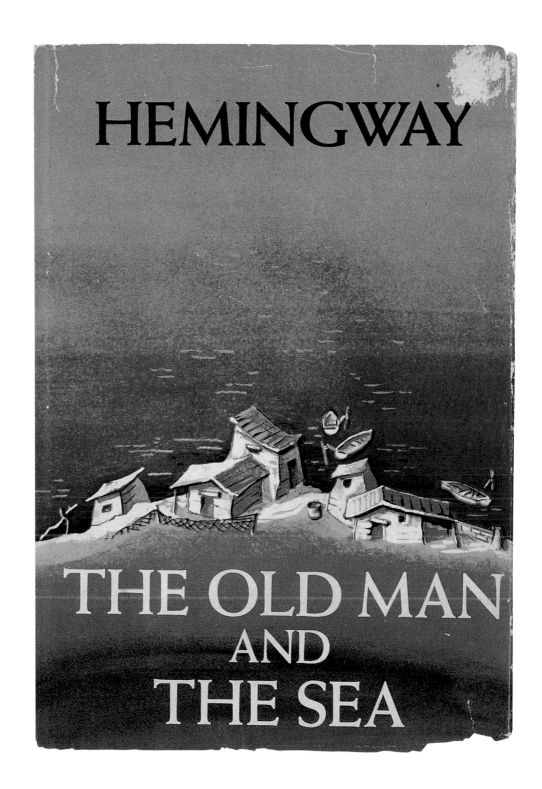

The Old Man and the Sea, 1952

Hemingway's confidence in his own work was sometimes misplaced, but not in the case of *The Old Man and the Sea*. Paying its author the handsome price of $40,000, *Life* magazine published the novella in toto in a single issue, and within forty-eight hours, all 5.3 million copies were snapped up. The *Life* publication did not lessen demand for the work in hardcover, and for six months it remained on the best-sellers list. Perhaps most noteworthy was the rapid acceptance of *The Old Man and the Sea* into the canon of American classics.

Private collection

Hemingway with Philip Percival and Denis Zaphiro on his African safari of 1953

In the photograph here, Hemingway sits in camp over morning coffee. On the right is Denis Zaphiro, a Kenya game ranger who acted as a chief guide to the safari. On the left is the expedition's leader, the veteran professional hunter Philip Percival. As a young man, Percival had been part of ex-President Theodore Roosevelt's much-publicized safari of 1910.

Earl Theisen (1903–73), gelatin silver print, 20.3 x 19 cm (8 x 7 ½ in.), 1953. Ernest Hemingway Collection, John F. Kennedy Library, Boston, Massachusetts. Copyright © 1998 Earl Theisen Archives

Hemingway at his writing desk during his African safari

This picture resonates with a stolid serenity, which belies the erratic behavior that sometimes characterized Hemingway on his 1953 safari. Drinking heavily, he took up with a native girl under the eyes of his wife; he shaved his head in the name of "going native"; and then, dyeing his clothes a rusty color to match the hue favored among the local Masai people, he went hunting with a spear.

Earl Theisen (1903–73), gelatin silver print, 18.7 x 19 cm (7 ⅜ x 7 ½ in.), 1953. Ernest Hemingway Collection, John F. Kennedy Library, Boston, Massachusetts. Copyright © 1998 Earl Theisen Archives

Remains of the airplane that crashed while carrying Hemingway and his wife on a sightseeing air tour of Africa

Hemingway closed his safari in late January 1954 with an airplane tour of some of the more spectacular natural sites in east Africa. Over Murchison Falls, the plane hit an abandoned telegraph wire, forcing it into a crash landing. Fortunately, Hemingway and his wife came out of the mishap only slightly hurt, and after an uneasy night in the jungle wilderness, they were rescued. But the adventure was not over. The day after the crash, as the plane that was to take the couple to Kampala, the capital of Uganda, was taxiing at a primitive airfield, it too crashed. This time, Hemingway was not so lucky, and he emerged from the wreck with multiple serious injuries, some of which would never heal.

The double misfortune, however, yielded a peculiar compensation. While Hemingway was lost in the jungle, it was reported that he was dead, and after the second crash, he had the eerie privilege of reading his own newspaper obituaries. A number of the pieces, alluding to his active sporting life and war experiences, claimed that he had always sought death. Hemingway responded, "Can one imagine if a man sought death all his life he could not have found her before the age of 54?"

Ernest Hemingway Collection, John F. Kennedy Library, Boston, Massachusetts [*Meyers, p. 506*]

Hemingway being awarded the Nobel Prize in literature

Hemingway had often professed disdain for the Nobel Prize in literature, and he claimed that too many of its recipients never wrote a worthwhile thing after getting it. But when it came his way in 1954, there was no doubt that he was pleased. Claiming ill health, he said he could not go to Sweden to accept the award. Instead, the Swedish ambassador to Cuba came to his home outside Havana to present him with the Nobel medal and citation.

Unidentified photographer, gelatin silver print, 19 x 17.2 cm (7 ½ x 6 ¾ in.), 1954.
Ernest Hemingway Collection, John F. Kennedy Library, Boston, Massachusetts

Hemingway during his last visit to Spain

In 1959 and 1960, Hemingway made extended trips to Spain and reimmersed himself in the world of bullfighting, the passion of his early days and the backdrop for his first major literary triumph, *The Sun Also Rises*. On the surface, the sojourns sometimes seemed like joyful royal progresses, as bullfighters dedicated their bulls to him and autograph seekers closed around him in adulation. But closer scrutiny revealed a man who was becoming increasingly erratic, irascible, and even cruel.

This radiantly sunny photograph portrait, taken during Hemingway's 1960 stay in Spain, might suggest that his stability on this trip was better than it had been the previous year. Unfortunately, that was not the case. Severely depressed, he was beginning to suffer from delusions and paranoia. Reflecting the inner turmoil was Hemingway's reaction when *Life* ran this likeness on its cover. To the world at large it was undeniably engaging; to Hemingway it was a "horrible face."

Loomis Dean (born 1917), photograph, 1960. Loomis Dean / Life magazine. Copyright © Time Inc. [Baker, Life Story, p. 554]

Hemingway opening presents at his sixtieth birthday celebration

On July 21, 1959, Hemingway turned sixty, and to mark that watershed, his wife Mary threw an elaborate party at the spacious home of a millionaire friend who was serving as their host during their stay in Spain. Beginning at noon and lasting until noon the next day, the celebration featured food flown in from London, fireworks, an orchestra, flamenco dancers, and a shooting booth where guests could test their marksmanship. Hemingway enjoyed himself, but the celebration produced some indications that all was not well with him. Among them was a nasty flash of ill temper directed at his frontline pal from World War II, General Buck Lanham. Having come from Washington for the party, he left Spain certain that Hemingway was a seriously troubled man.

Unidentified photographer, gelatin silver print, 14.3 x 16.8 cm (4 ⅝ x 6 ⅝ in.), 1959.
Ernest Hemingway Collection, John F. Kennedy Library, Boston, Massachusetts

Hemingway's funeral in Ketchum, Idaho, July 5, 1961

Hemingway's mental state worsened drastically in the fall of 1960, and at the end of November, he was taken to the Mayo Clinic in Rochester, Minnesota, where his severe depression was treated with electric shock therapy. By late January he was judged well enough for release. But soon after returning to his home in Ketchum, Idaho, his condition worsened, and he was checked back into the Mayo late in April 1961 to undergo further shock therapy. Again he seemed to get better, and in late June he was released. In the early morning, two days after arriving home, he took one of his hunting rifles from basement storage and shot himself.

Francis Miller (active 1950s and 1960s), photograph, 1961. Francis Miller / Life magazine. Copyright © Time Inc.

SELECTED BIBLIOGRAPHY

Baker, Carlos. *Ernest Hemingway: A Life Story.* New York: Scribner, 1969.

———, ed. *Ernest Hemingway: Selected Letters.* New York: Scribner, 1981.

Berg, A. Scott. *Max Perkins: Editor of Genius.* New York: Dutton, 1978.

Brian, Denis. *The True Gen: An Intimate Portrait of Ernest Hemingway by Those Who Knew Him.* New York: Grove, 1987.

Bruccoli, Matthew J. *Scott and Ernest.* Carbondale: Southern Illinois University Press, 1978.

———. *Some Sort of Epic Grandeur.* New York: Harcourt Brace Jovanovich, 1981.

———, ed. *The Only Thing That Counts: The Ernest Hemingway / Maxwell Perkins Correspondence, 1925–1947.* New York: Scribner, 1996.

Carr, Virginia Spencer. *Dos Passos: A Life.* Garden City, N.Y.: Doubleday, 1984.

Diliberto, Gioia. *Hadley.* New York: Ticknor and Fields, 1992.

Fenton, Charles A. *The Apprenticeship of Ernest Hemingway.* New York: Farrar, Straus and Young, 1954.

Fitch, Noel Riley. *Sylvia Beach and the Lost Generation.* New York: Norton, 1983.

Hanneman, Audre. *Ernest Hemingway: A Comprehensive Bibliography.* Princeton, N.J.: Princeton University Press, 1967.

Hemingway, Ernest. *A Moveable Feast.* New York: Scribner, 1964.

Hemingway, Mary Welsh. *How It Was.* New York: Knopf, 1976.

Lynn, Kenneth S. *Hemingway.* New York: Simon and Schuster, 1987.

Mellow, James R. *Invented Lives: F. Scott and Zelda Fitzgerald.* Boston: Houghton Mifflin, 1984.

———. *Hemingway: A Life Without Consequences.* Boston: Houghton Mifflin, 1992.

Meyers, Jeffrey. *Hemingway: A Biography.* New York: Harper and Row, 1985.

Raeburn, John. *Fame Became of Him: Hemingway as Public Writer.* Bloomington: Indiana University Press, 1984.

Reynolds, Michael. *Hemingway's First War.* Princeton, N.J.: Princeton University Press, 1976.

———. *The Young Hemingway.* New York: Blackwell, 1986.

———. *Hemingway: The Paris Years.* Cambridge, Mass.: Blackwell, 1989.

———. *Hemingway: The American Homecoming.* Cambridge, Mass.: Blackwell, 1992.

———. *Hemingway: The 1930s.* New York: Norton, 1997.

———. *Hemingway: The Final Years.* New York: Norton, 1999.

Sokoloff, Alice Hunt. *Hadley: The First Mrs. Hemingway*. New York: Dodd, Mead, 1973.

Stein, Gertrude. *The Autobiography of Alice B. Toklas*. New York: Harcourt, Brace, 1933.

Watts, Emily Stipes. *Ernest Hemingway and the Arts*. Urbana: University of Illinois Press, 1971.

PHOTOGRAPHY CREDITS

Don Gair, Kittery, Maine: pp. 14, 15

Rolland White: pp. 26, 65, 66, 72, 75, 89, 97

DISPLAY PHOTOGRAPHS AND DETAILS

For p. i credit see p. 45; p. ii, see p. 99; p. vi, see p. 53; p. x, see p. 57; p. xii, see p. 102; p. 1, see p. 23; p. 10, see p. 86; p. 13, see p. 33; p. 50, see p. 74.

INDEX

EH in the entries stands for Ernest Hemingway.
Page numbers in **bold type** denote an image, and
may reference either the artist or the subject.